Queen Hortense
A Life Picture of the Napoleonic Era
Book III
THE RESTORATION

by

L. Mühlbach

Double 9
BOOKS

Queen Hortense
A Life Picture of the Napoleonic Era
Book III
THE RESTORATION
by L. Mühlbach

ISBN: 978-93-64281-24-9

Published by

DOUBLE 9 BOOKS

2/13-B, Ansari Road
Daryaganj, New Delhi – 110002
info@double9books.com
www.double9books.com
Tel. 011-40042856

ABOUT THE AUTHOR

Louise Mühlbach, the pen name of Clara Mundt (1814-1873), was a prolific German author renowned for her historical novels. Born on January 2, 1814, in Neubrandenburg, Mecklenburg-Schwerin, Germany, she married Theodore Mundt, a literary critic and author. This marriage significantly influenced her literary career, providing her with access to intellectual circles and literary discussions of the time. Mühlbach is best known for her novels that vividly depict 18th-century and 19th-century European history. She adeptly blended historical facts with fictionalized personal drama, making her works both engaging and accessible. Some of her most notable novels include "Joseph II and His Court," "Frederick the Great and His Court," "Marie Antoinette and Her Son," and "Old Fritz and the New Era." These novels often focused on significant historical figures and events, bringing them to life through vivid characterizations and intricate plots. Mühlbach 's novels are characterized by rich historical detail, though she often took creative liberties with facts for dramatic effect. Her works reflect the intellectual currents of her time, particularly the influences of the Enlightenment and Romanticism. She emphasized themes of individualism, heroism, and the complexities of historical change.

During her lifetime, Mühlbach's novels were widely read and translated into several languages, making her one of the most popular authors of historical fiction in the 19th century. Despite mixed reviews from critics, who sometimes criticized her for historical inaccuracies and melodramatic elements, her ability to blend historical events with engaging narratives had a lasting impact on the genre.

CONTENTS

CHAPTER I
THE RETURN OF THE BOURBONS

On the 12th of April, Count d'Artois, whom Louis XVIII. had sent in advance, and invested with the dignity of a lieutenant-general of France, made his triumphal entry into Paris. At the gates of the city, he was received by the newly-formed provisional government, Talleyrand at its head; and here it was that Count d'Artois replied to the address of that gentleman in the following words: "Nothing is changed in France, except that from to-day there will be one Frenchman more in the land." The people received him with cold curiosity, and the allied troops formed a double line for his passage to the Tuileries, at which the ladies of the Faubourg St. Germain, adorned with white lilies and white cockades, received him with glowing enthusiasm. Countess Ducayla, afterward the well-known friend of Louis XVIII., had been one of the most active instruments of the restoration, and she it was who had first unfolded again in France the banner of the Bourbons--the white flag. A few days before the entrance of the prince, she had gone, with a number of her royalist friends, into the streets, in order to excite the people to some enthusiasm for the legitimate dynasty. But the people and the army had still preserved their old love for the emperor, and the proclamation of Prince Schwartzenberg, read by Bauvineux in the streets, was listened to in silence. True, the royalists cried, *"Vive le roi!"* at the end of this reading, but the people remained indifferent and mute.

This sombre silence alarmed Countess Ducayla; it seemed to indicate a secret discontent with the new order of things. She felt that this sullen people must be inflamed, and made to speak with energy and distinctness. To awaken enthusiasm by means of words and proclamations had been attempted in vain; now the countess determined to attempt to arouse them by another means--to astonish them by the display of a striking symbol--to show them the white flag of the Bourbons!

She gave her companion, Count de Montmorency, her handkerchief, that he might wave it aloft, fastening it to the end of his cane, in order that it should be more conspicuous. This handkerchief of Countess Ducayla, fastened to the cane of a Montmorency, was the first royalist banner that fluttered over Paris, after a banishment of twenty years. The Parisians looked at this banner with a kind of reverence and shuddering wonder; they did not greet it with applause; they still remained silent, but they nevertheless followed the procession of royalists, who marched to the boulevards, shouting, *"Vive le roi!"* They took no part in their joyful demonstration, but neither did they attempt to prevent it.

This demonstration of the royalists, and particularly of the royalist ladies, transcended the bounds of propriety, and of their own dignity. In their fanaticism for the legitimate dynasty, they gave the allies a reception, which almost assumed the character of a declaration of love, on the part of the fair ladies of the Faubourg St. Germain, for all the soldiers and officers of the allied army. In a strange confusion of ideas, these warriors, who had certainly entered France as enemies, seemed to these fair ones to be a part of the beloved Bourbons; and they loved them with almost the same love they lavished upon the royal family itself. During several days they were, in their hearts, the daughters of all countries except their own!

Louis XVIII. was himself much displeased with this enthusiasm of the ladies of the Faubourg St. Germain, and openly avowed to Countess Ducayla his dissatisfaction with the ridiculous and contemptible behavior of these ladies at that time. He was even of the opinion that it was calculated to injure his cause, as the nation had then not yet pronounced in his favor.

"They should," said he, "have received the allies with a dignified reserve, without frivolous demonstrations, and without this inconsiderate devotion. Such a demeanor would have inspired them with respect for the nation, whereas they now leave Paris with the conviction that we are still--as we were fifty years ago--the most giddy and frivolous people of Europe. You particularly, ladies--you have compromised yourselves in an incomprehensible manner. The allies seemed to you so lovable *en masse,* that you gave yourselves the appearance of also loving them *en détail;* and this has occasioned reports concerning you which do little honor to French ladies!"

"But, *mon Dieu!*" replied Countess Ducayla to her royal friend, "we wished to show them a well-earned gratitude for the benefit they conferred in restoring to us your majesty; we wished to offer them freely what we, tired of resistance, were at last compelled to accord to the tyrants of the republic and the sabre-heroes of the empire! None of us can regret what we have done for our good friends the allies!"

Nevertheless, that which the ladies "had done for their good friends the allies" was the occasion of many annoying family scenes, and the husbands who did not fully participate in the enthusiasm of their wives were of the opinion that they had good cause to complain of their inordinate zeal.

Count G----, among others, had married a young and beautiful lady a few days before the restoration. She, in her youthful innocence, was entirely indifferent to political matters; but her step-father, her step-mother, and her husband, Count G----, were royalists of the first water.

On the day of the entrance of the allies into Paris, step-father, step-mother, and husband, in common with all good legitimists, hurried forward to welcome "their good friends," and each of them returned to their dwelling with a stranger--the husband with an Englishman, the step-mother with a Prussian, and the step-father with an Austrian. The three endeavored to outdo each other in the attentions which they showered upon the guests they had the good fortune to possess. The little countess alone remained indifferent, in the midst of the joy of her family. They reproached her with having too little attachment for the good cause, and exhorted her to do everything in her power to entertain the gallant men who had restored to France her king.

The husband requested the Englishman to instruct the young countess in riding; the marquise begged the Prussian to escort her daughter to the ball, and teach her the German waltz; and, finally, the marquis, who had discovered a fine taste for paintings in the Austrian, appealed to this gentleman to conduct the young wife through the picture-galleries.

In short, every opportunity was given the young countess to commit a folly, or rather three follies, for she did not like to give the preference to any one of the three strangers. She was young, and inexperienced in matters of this kind. Her triple intrigue was, therefore, soon discovered, and betrayed to her family; and now husband, step-father, and step-mother, were exasperated. This exceeded even the demands of their royalism; and they showered reproaches on the head of the young wife.

"It is not my fault!" cried she, sobbing. "I only did what you commanded. You ordered me to do everything in my power to entertain these gentlemen, and I could therefore refuse them nothing."

But there were also cases in which the advances of the enthusiastic ladies of the Faubourg St. Germain were repelled. Even the high-born and haughty Marquise M---- was to experience this mortification. She stepped before the sullen, sombre veterans of the Old Guard of the empire, who had just allowed Count d'Artois to pass before their ranks in dead silence. She ardently appealed to their love for the dynasty of their fathers, and, in her enthusiasm for royalism, went so far as to offer herself as a reward to him who should first cry *"Vive le roi!"* But the faithful soldiers of the emperor stood unmoved by this generous offer, and the silence remained unbroken by the lowest cry!

The princes who stood at the head of the allied armies were, of course, the objects of the most ardent enthusiasm of the royalist ladies; but it was, above all, with them that they found the least encouragement. The Emperor of Austria was too much occupied with the future of his daughter and grandson, and the King of Prussia was too grave and severe, to find any pleasure in the coquetries of women. The young Emperor Alexander of Russia, therefore, became the chief object of their enthusiasm and love. But their enthusiasm also met with a poor recompense in this quarter. Almost distrustfully, the czar held himself aloof from the ladies of the Faubourg St. Germain; and yet it was they who had decided the fate of France with him, and induced him to give his vote for the Bourbons; for until then it had remained undetermined whom the allies should call to the throne of France.

In his inmost heart, the Emperor of Russia desired to see the universally-beloved Viceroy of Italy, Eugene Beauharnais, elevated to the vacant throne. The letter with which Eugene replied to the proposition of the allies, tendering him the ducal crown of Genoa, had won for Josephine's son the love and esteem of the czar for all time. Alexander had himself written to Eugene, and proffered him, in the name of the allies, a duchy of Genoa, if he would desert Napoleon, and take sides with the allies. Eugene Beauharnais had replied to him in the following letter:

"SIRE,--I have received your majesty's propositions. They are undoubtedly very favorable, but they are powerless to change my resolution. I must have known how to express my thoughts but poorly when I had the honor of seeing you, if your majesty can believe that I could sully my honor for any, even the highest, reward. Neither the prospect of possessing the crown of the duchy of Genoa, nor that of the kingdom of Italy, can induce me to become a traitor. The example of the King of Naples cannot mislead me; I will rather be a plain soldier than a traitorous prince.

"The emperor, you say, has done me injustice; I have forgotten it; I only remember his benefits. I owe all to him--my rank, my titles, and my fortune, and I owe to him that which I prefer to all else--that which your indulgence calls my renown. I shall, therefore, serve him as long as I live; my person is his, as is my heart. May my sword break in my hands, if it could ever turn against the emperor, or against France! I trust that my well-grounded refusal will at least secure to me the respect of your imperial majesty. I am, etc."

The Emperor of Austria, on the other hand, ardently desired to secure the throne of France to his grandson, the King of Rome, under the regency of the Empress Marie Louise; but he did not venture to make this demand openly and without reservation of his allies, whose action he had promised to approve and ratify. The appeals of the Duke of Cadore, who had been sent to her father by Marie Louise from Blois, urging the emperor to look after her interests, and to demand of the allies that they should assure the crown to herself and son, were, therefore, fruitless.

The emperor assured his daughter's ambassador that he had reason to hope for the best for her, but that he was powerless to insist on any action in her behalf.

"I love my daughter," said the good emperor, "and I love my son-in-law, and I am ready to shed my heart's blood for them."

"Majesty," said the duke, interrupting him, "no such sacrifice is required at your hands."

"I am ready to shed my blood for them," continued the emperor, "to sacrifice my life for them, and I repeat it, I have promised the allies to do nothing except in conjunction with them, and to consent to all they determine. Moreover, my minister, Count Metternich, is at this moment with them, and I shall ratify everything which he has signed[30]."

[30] Bourrienne, vol. x., p. 129.

But the emperor still hoped that that which Metternich should sign for him, would be the declaration that the little King of Rome was to be the King of France.

But the zeal of the royalists was destined to annihilate this hope.

The Emperor of Russia had now taken up his residence in Talleyrand's house. He had yielded to the entreaties of the shrewd French diplomat, who well knew how much easier it would be to bend the will of the Agamemnon of the holy alliance[31] to his wishes, when he should have him in hand, as it were, day and night. In offering the emperor his hospitality, it was

Talleyrand's intention to make him his prisoner, body and soul, and to use him to his own advantage.

[31] Mémoires d'une Femme de Qualité.

It was therefore to Talleyrand that Countess Ducayla hastened to concert measures with the Bonapartist of yesterday, who had transformed himself into the zealous legitimist of to-day.

Talleyrand undertook to secure the countess an audience with the Russian emperor, and he succeeded.

While conducting the beautiful countess to the czar's cabinet, Talleyrand whispered in her ear: "Imitate Madame de Lemallé--endeavor to make a great stroke. The emperor is gallant, and what he denies to diplomacy he may, perhaps, accord to the ladies."

He left her at the door, and the countess entered the emperor's cabinet alone. She no sooner saw him, than she sank on her knees, and stretched out her arms.

With a knightly courtesy, the emperor immediately hastened forward to assist her to rise.

"What are you doing?" asked he, almost in alarm. "A noble lady never has occasion to bend the knee to a cavalier."

"Sire," exclaimed the countess, "I kneel before you, because it is my purpose to implore of your majesty the happiness which you alone can restore to us; it will be a double pleasure to possess Louis XVIII. once more, when Alexander I. shall have given him to us!"

"Is it then true that the French people are still devoted to the Bourbon family?"

"Yes, sire, they are our only hope; on them we bestow our whole love!"

"Ah, that is excellent," cried Alexander; "are all French ladies filled with the same enthusiasm as yourself, madame?"

"Well, if this is the case, it will be France that recalls Louis XVIII., and it will not be necessary for us to conduct him back. Let the legislative bodies declare their will, and it shall be done[32]."

[32] Mémoires d'une Femme de Qualité, vol. i., p. 179.

And of all women, Countess Ducayla was the one to bring the legislative bodies to the desired declaration. She hastened to communicate the hopes with which the emperor had inspired her to all Paris; on the evening after her interview with the emperor, she gave a grand *soirée*, to which she invited the most beautiful ladies of her party, and a number of senators.

"I desired by this means," says she in her memoirs, "to entrap the gentlemen into making a vow. How simple-minded I was! Did I not know that the majority of them had already made and broken a dozen vows?"

On the following day the senate assembled, and elected a provisional government, consisting of Talleyrand, the Duke of Dalberg, the Marquis of Jancourt, Count Bournonville, and the Abbé Montesquieu. The senate and the new provisional government thereupon declared Napoleon deposed from the throne, and recalled Louis XVIII. But while the senate thus publicly and solemnly proclaimed its legitimist sentiments in the name of the French people, it at the same time testified to its own unworthiness and selfishness. In the treaty made by the senate with its recalled king, it was provided in a separate clause, "that the salary which they had hitherto received, should be continued to them for life." While recalling Louis XVIII., these senators took care to pay themselves for their trouble, and to secure their own future.

CHAPTER II
THE BOURBONS AND THE BONAPARTES

The allies hastened to consider the declaration of the senate and provisional government as the declaration of the people, and recalled to the throne of his fathers Louis XVIII., who, as Count de Lille, had so long languished in exile at Hartwell.

The Emperor of Austria kept his word; he made no resistance to the decrees of his allies, and allowed his grandson, the King of Rome, to be robbed of his inheritance, and the imperial crown to fall from his daughter's brow. The Emperor Francis was, however, as much astonished at this result as Marie Louise, for, until their entrance into Paris, the allies had flattered the Austrian emperor with the hope that the crown of France would be secured to his daughter and grandson. The emperor's astonishment at this turn of affairs was made the subject of a caricature, which, on the day of the entrance of Louis XVIIL, was affixed to the same walls on which Chateaubriand's enthusiastic *brochure* concerning the Bourbons was posted. In this caricature, of which thousands of copies were sown broadcast throughout Paris, the Emperor of Austria was to be seen sitting in an elegant open carriage; the Emperor Alexander sat on the coachman's box, the Regent of England as postilion on the lead-horse, and the King of Prussia stood up behind as a lackey. Napoleon ran along on foot at the side of the carriage, holding fast to it, and crying out to the Emperor of Austria, "Father-in-law, they have thrown me out"--"And *taken me in*," was the reply of Francis I.

The exultation of the ladies of the Faubourg St. Germain was great, now that their king was at last restored to them, and they eagerly embraced every means of showing their gratitude to the Emperor of Russia. But Alexander remained entirely insusceptible to their homage; he even went so far as to avoid attending the entertainments given by the new king at the Tuileries, and society was shocked at seeing the emperor openly displaying his sympathy for the family of the Emperor Napoleon, and repairing to Malmaison, instead of appearing at the Tuileries.

Count Nesselrode at last conjured his friend Louise de Cochelet to inform the czar of the feeling of dismay that pervaded the Faubourg St.

Germain, when he should come to Queen Hortense's maid-of-honor, as he was in the habit of doing from time to time, for the purpose of discussing the queen's interests with her.

"Sire," said she to the czar, "the Faubourg St. Germain regards your majesty's zeal in the queen's behalf with great jealousy. It has even caused Count Nesselrode much concern. 'Our emperor,' said he to me, recently, 'goes to Malmaison much too often; the high circles of society, and the diplomatic body, are already in dismay about it; it is feared that he is there subjected to influences to which policy requires he should not be exposed.'"

"This is characteristic of my Nesselrode," replied the emperor, laughing, "he is so easily disquieted. What do I care for the Faubourg St. Germain? It speaks ill enough for these ladies that they have not made a conquest of me! I prefer the noble qualities of the soul to all outward appearances; and I find united in the Empress Josephine, in the Queen of Holland, and in Prince Eugene, all that is admirable and lovable. I am better pleased to be here with you in quiet, confidential intercourse, than with those who really demean themselves as though they were crazed, and who, instead of enjoying the triumph we have prepared for them, are only intent on destroying their enemies, and have commenced with those who formerly accorded them such generous protection; they really weary one with their extravagances."

"Frenchwomen are coquettish," said the emperor in the course of the conversation; "I came here in great fear of them, for I knew how far their amiability could extend; but their heart is undoubtedly no longer their own. I am therefore on my guard against being deceived by it, and I fancy these ladies love to please so well, that they are even angry with those who respond to the attentions which are so lavishly showered on them, with conventional politeness only."

Louise de Cochelet undertook to defend the French ladies against the emperor's attacks. She told him he should not judge of them by the manner in which they had conducted themselves toward him, as it was but natural that the ladies should be inspired with enthusiasm for a young emperor who appeared to them in so favorable a light, and that they must necessarily, even without being coquettish, ardently desire to be noticed by him.

"But," said the emperor, with his soft, sad smile, "have these ladies only been waiting for me in order to feel their heart palpitate? I seek mind and entertainment, but I fly from all those who display a desire to exercise a control over my heart; in this I see nothing but self-love, and I hold myself aloof from such contact."

While the royalists and the ladies of the Faubourg St. Germain were lavishing attentions upon the allies, and assuring the returned king of the boundless delight of his people, this people was already beginning to grumble. The allies had now completed their task, they had restored to France its legitimate king, and they now put the finishing-touch to their work by providing in the treaty, that France should be narrowed down to the boundaries it had had before the revolution.

France was compelled to conform to the will of its vanquishers. From the weakness of the legitimists they now snatched that which they had been compelled to accord to the strength of the empire.

All of those fortified places, that had been bought with so much French blood, and that were still held by Frenchmen, were to be given up, and the great, extended France was to shrink back into the France it had been thirty years before! It was this that made the people murmur. The Frenchmen who had left Napoleon because they had grown weary of endless wars, were, nevertheless, proud of the conquests they had made under their emperor. The surrender of these conquests wounded the national pride, and they were angry with their king for being so ready to put this shame upon France--for holding the crown of France in higher estimation than the honor of France!

It must be conceded, however, that Louis XVIII. had most bitterly felt the disgrace that attached to him in this re-establishment of France within its ancient boundaries, and he had endeavored to protest in every way against this demand of the allies. But his representative had been made to understand that if Louis XVIII. could not content himself with the France the allies were prepared to give him, he was at liberty to relinquish it to Marie Louise. The king was, therefore, compelled to yield to necessity; but he did so with bitter mortification, and while his courtiers were giving free rein to their enthusiasm for the allies, he was heard to whisper, "*Nos chers amis les ennemis* [33]!"

[33] "Our dear friends the enemies!"

Thus embittered against the allies, it was only with great reluctance, and after a long and bitter struggle, that Louis XVIII. consented to the demands made by the allies in behalf of the family of Napoleon. But the Emperor Alexander kept his word; he defended the rights of the Queen of Holland and her children against the ill-will of the Bourbons, the dislike of the royalists, and the disinclination of the allies, alike. The family of the emperor owed it to him and to his firmness alone that the article of the treaty of the 11th of April, in which Louis XVIII. agreed "that the titles and dignities of all the members of the family of the Emperor Napoleon should be recognized, and that they should not be deprived of them," remained something more than a mere phrase.

It was only after repeated efforts that the emperor at last succeeded in obtaining for Hortense, from Louis XVIII., an estate and a title, that secured her position. King Louis finally yielded to his urgent solicitations, and conferred upon Hortense the title of Duchess of St. Leu, and made her estate, St. Leu, a duchy.

But this was done with the greatest reluctance, and only under the pressure of the king's obligations to the allies, who had given him his throne; and these obligations the Bourbons would have forgotten as willingly as the whole period of the revolution and of the empire.

For the Bourbons seemed but to have awakened from a long sleep, and were not a little surprised to find that the world had progressed in the meanwhile.

According to their ideas, every thing must have remained standing at the point where they had left it twenty years before; and they were at least determined to ignore all that had happened in the interval. King Louis therefore signed his first act as in "the nineteenth" year of his reign, and endeavored in all things to keep up a semblance of the continuation of his reign since the year 1789. Hence, the letters-patent in which King Louis appointed Hortense Duchess of St. Leu were drawn up in a manner offensive to the queen, for they contained the following: "The king appoints Mademoiselle Hortense de Beauharnais Duchess of St. Leu."

The queen refused to accept this title, under the circumstances, and rejected the letters-patent. It was not until the czar had angrily demanded it, that M. de Blacas, the king's premier, consented to draw up the letters-patent in a different style. They read: "The king appoints Hortense Eugénie, included in the treaty of the 11th of April, Duchess of St. Leu." This was, to be sure, merely a negative and disguised recognition of the former rank of the queen; but it was, at least no longer a degradation to accept it.

The Viceroy of Italy, the noble Eugene--who was universally beloved, and who had come to Paris, at the express wish of the czar, to secure his future--occasioned the Bourbons quite as much annoyance and perplexity.

The king could not refuse to recognize the brave hero of the empire and the son-in-law of the King of Bavaria, who was one of the allies; and, as Eugene desired an audience of the king, it was accorded him at once.

But how was he to be received? With what title was Napoleon's step-son, the Viceroy of Italy, to be addressed? It would have been altogether too ridiculous to repeat the absurdity contained in Hortense's letters-patent, and call Eugene "Viscount de Beauharnais;" but to accord him the royal title would have compromised the dignity of the legitimate dynasty. A brilliant solution of this difficult question suggested itself to King Louis. When the Duke d'Aumont conducted Prince Eugene to the royal presence, the king advanced, with a cordial smile, and saluted him with the words, "M. Marshal of France, I am happy to see you."

Eugene, who was on the point of making his salutation, remained silent, and looked over his shoulder to see whom the king was speaking with. Louis XVIII. smiled, and continued: "You, my dear sir, are a marshal of France. I appoint you to this dignity."

"Sire," said Eugene, bowing profoundly, "I am much obliged to your majesty for your kind intentions, but the misfortune of the rank to which destiny has called me will not allow me to accept the high title with which you honor me. I thank you very much, but I must decline it[34]."

[34] Mémoires d'une Femme de Qualité, vol. i., p. 267.

The king's stratagem had thus come to grief, and Eugene left the royal presence with flying colors. He was not under the necessity of accepting benefits from the King of France, for his step-father, the King of Bavaria, made Eugene a prince of the royal house of Bavaria, and created for him the duchy of Leuchtenberg. Hither Eugene retired, and lived there, surrounded by his wife and children, in peace and tranquillity, until death tore him from the arms of his sorrowing family, in the year 1824.

CHAPTER III
MADAME DE STAËL

The restoration, that had overthrown so many of the great, and that was destined to restore to the light so many names that had lain buried in obscurity, now brought back to Paris a person who had been banished by Napoleon, and who had been adding new lustre and renown to her name in a foreign land. This personage was Madame de Staël, the daughter of Necker, the renowned poetess of "Corinne" and "Delphine."

It had been a long and bitter struggle between Madame de Staël and the mighty Emperor of the French; and Madame de Staël, with her genius and her impassioned eloquence, and adorned with the laurel-wreath of her exile, had perhaps done Napoleon more harm than a whole army of his enemies. Intense hatred existed on both sides, and yet it had depended on Napoleon alone to transform this hatred into love. For Madame de Staël had been disposed to lavish the whole impassioned enthusiasm of her heart upon the young hero of Marengo and Arcola--quite disposed to become the Egeria of this Numa Pompilius. In the warm impulse of her stormy imagination, Madame de Staël, in reference to Bonaparte, had even, in a slight measure, been regardless of her position as a lady, and had only remembered that she was a poetess, and that, as such, it became her well to celebrate the hero, and to bestow on the luminous constellation that was rising over France the glowing dithyrambic of her greetings.

Portrait of Madame de Staël.

Madame de Staël had, therefore, not waited for Napoleon to seek her, but had made the first advances, and sought him.

To the returning victor of Italy she wrote letters filled with impassioned enthusiasm; but these letters afforded the youthful general but little pleasure. In the midst of the din of battle and the grand schemes with which he was continually engaged, Bonaparte found but little time to occupy himself with the poetical works of Madame de Staël. He knew of her nothing more than that she was the daughter of the minister Necker, and that was no recommendation in Napoleon's eyes, for he felt little respect for Necker's genius, and even went so far as to call him the instigator of the great revolution. It was, therefore, with astonishment that the young general received the enthusiastic letter of the poetess; and, while showing it to some of his intimate friends, he said, with a shrug of his shoulders, "Do you understand these extravagances? This woman is foolish!"

But Madame de Staël did not allow herself to be dismayed by Bonaparte's coldness and silence--she continued to write new and more glowing letters.

In one of these letters she went so far in her inconsiderate enthusiasm as to say, that it was a great error in human institutions that the gentle and quiet Josephine had united her faith with his; that she, Madame de Staël, and Bonaparte, were born for each other, and that Nature seemed to have created a soul of fire like hers, in order that it might worship a hero such as he was.

Bonaparte crushed the letter in his hands, and exclaimed, as he threw it in the fire: "That a blue-stocking, a manufactress of sentiment, should dare to compare herself to Josephine! I shall not answer these letters!"

He did not answer them, but Madame de Staël did not, or rather would not, understand his silence. Little disposed to give up a resolution once formed, and to see her plans miscarry, Madame de Staël was now also determined to have her way, and to approach Bonaparte despite his resistance.

And she did have her way; she succeeded in overcoming all obstacles, and the interview, so long wished for by her, and so long avoided by him, at last took place. Madame de Staël was introduced at the Tuileries, and received by Bonaparte and his wife. The personal appearance of this intellectual woman was, however, but little calculated to overcome Bonaparte's prejudice. The costume of Madame de Staël was on this occasion, as it always was, fantastic, and utterly devoid of taste, and Napoleon loved to see women simply but elegantly and tastefully attired. In this interview with Napoleon, Madame de Staël gave free scope to her wit; but instead of dazzling him, as she had hoped to do, she only succeeded in depressing him.

It was while in this frame of mind, and when Madame de Staël, in her ardor, had endeavored almost to force him to pay her a compliment, that Napoleon responded to her at least somewhat indiscreet question: "Who is in your eyes the greatest woman?" with the sarcastic reply, "She who bears the most children to the state."

Madame de Staël had come with a heart full of enthusiasm; in her address to Napoleon, she had called him a "god descended to earth;" she had come an enthusiastic poetess; she departed an offended woman. Her wounded vanity never forgave the answer which seemed to make her ridiculous. She avenged herself, in her drawing-room, by the biting *bon mots* which she hurled at Napoleon and his family, and which were of course faithfully repeated to the first consul.

But the weapons which this intellectual woman now wielded against the hero who had scorned her, wounded him more severely than weapons of steel or iron. In the use of these weapons, Madame de Staël was his superior, and the consciousness of this embittered Bonaparte all the more against the lady, who dared prick the heel of Achilles with the needle of her wit, and strike at the very point where he was most sensitive.

A long and severe conflict now began between these two greatest geniuses of that period, a struggle that was carried on by both with equal bitterness. But Napoleon had outward power on his side, and could punish the enmity of his witty opponent, as a ruler.

He banished Madame de Staël from Paris, and soon afterward even from France. She who in Paris had been so ready to sing the praises of her "god descended from heaven," now went into exile his enemy and a royalist, to engage, with all her eloquence and genius, in making proselytes for the exiled Bourbons, and to raise in the minds of men an invisible but none the less formidable army against her enemy the great Napoleon.

Madame de Staël soon gave still greater weight to the flaming eruptions of her hatred of Napoleon, by her own increasing renown and greatness; and the poetess of Corinne and Delphine soon became as redoubtable an opponent of Napoleon as England, Russia, or Austria, could be.

But in the midst of the triumphs she was celebrating in her exile, Madame de Staël soon began to long ardently to return to France, which she loved all the more for having been compelled to leave it. She therefore used all the influence she possessed in Paris, to obtain from Napoleon permission to return to her home, but the emperor remained inexorable, even after having read Delphine.

"I love," said he, "women who make men of themselves just as little as I love effeminate men. There is an appropriate *rôle* for every one in the world. Of what use is this vagabondizing of fantasy? What does it accomplish? Nothing! All this is nothing but do rangement of mind and feeling. I dislike women who throw themselves in my arms, and for this reason, if for no other, I dislike this woman, who is certainly one of that number."

Madame de Staël's petitions to be permitted to return to Paris were therefore rejected, but she was as little disposed to abandon her purpose now as she was at the time she sought to gain Bonaparte's good-will. She continued to make attempts to achieve her aim, for it was not only her country that she wished to reconquer, but also a million francs which she wished to have paid to her out of the French treasury.

Her father, Minister Necker, had loaned his suffering country a million francs, at a time of financial distress and famine, to buy bread for the starving people, and Louis XVI. had guaranteed, in writing, that this "national debt of France" should be returned.

But the revolution that shattered the throne of the unfortunate king, also buried beneath the ruins of the olden time the promises and oaths that had been written on parchment and paper.

Madame de Staël now demanded that the emperor should fulfil the promises of the overthrown king, and that the heir of the throne of the Bourbons should assume the obligations into which a Bourbon had entered with her father.

She had once called Napoleon a god descended from heaven; and she even now wished that he might still prove a god for her, namely, the god Pluto, who should pour out a million upon her from his horn of plenty.

As she could not go to France herself, she sent her son to plead with the emperor, for herself and her children.

Well knowing, however, how difficult it would be, even for her son to secure an audience of the emperor, she addressed herself to Queen Hortense in eloquent letters imploring her to exert her influence in her son's behalf.

Hortense, ever full of pity for misfortune, felt the warmest sympathy and admiration for the genius of the great poetess, and interceded for Madame de Staël with great courage and eloquence. She alone ventured, regardless of Napoleon's frowns and displeasure, to plead the cause of the poor exile again and again, and to solicit her recall to France, as a simple act of justice; she even went so far in her generosity as to extend the hospitalities of her drawing-rooms to the poetess's son, who was avoided and fled from by every one else.

Hortense's soft entreaties and representations were at last successful in soothing the emperor's anger. He allowed Madame de Staël to return to France, on the condition that she should never come to Paris or its vicinity; he then also accorded Madame de Staël's son the long-sought favor of an audience.

This interview of Napoleon with Madame de Staël's son is as remarkable as it is original. On this occasion, Napoleon openly expressed his dislike and even his hatred as well of Madame de Staël as of her father, although he listened with generous composure to the warm defence of the son and grandson.

Young Staël told the emperor of his mother's longing to return to her home, and touchingly portrayed the sadness and unhappiness of her exile.

"Ah, bah!" exclaimed the emperor, "your mother is in a state of exaltation. I do not say that she is a bad woman. She has wit, and much intellect, perhaps too much, but hers is an inconsiderate, an insubordinate spirit. She has grown up in the chaos of a falling monarchy, and of a revolution, and she has amalgamized the two in her mind. This is all a source of danger; she would make proselytes, she must be watched; she does not love me. The interests of those whom she might compromise, require that I should not permit her to return to Paris. If I should allow her to do so, she would place me under the necessity of sending her to Bicétre, or of imprisoning her in the Temple, before six months elapsed; that would be extremely disagreeable, for it would cause a sensation, and injure me in the public opinion. Inform your mother that my resolution is irrevocable. While I live, she shall not return to Paris."

It was in vain that young Staël assured him in his mother's name, that she would avoid giving him the least occasion for displeasure, and that she would live in complete retirement if permitted to return to Paris.

"Ah, yes! I know the value of fine promises!" exclaimed the emperor. "I know what the result would be, and I repeat it, it cannot be! She would be the rallying-point of the whole Faubourg St. Germain. She live in retirement! Visits would be made her, and she would return them; she would commit a thousand indiscretions, and say a thousand humorous things, to which she attaches no importance, but which annoy me. My government is no jest, I take every thing seriously; I wish this to be understood, and you may proclaim it to the whole world!"

Young Staël had, however, the courage to continue his entreaties; he even went so far as to inquire in all humility for the grounds of the emperor's ill-will against his mother. He said he had been assured that Necker's last work was more particularly the cause of the emperor's displeasure, and that he believed Madame de Staël had assisted in writing it. This was, however, not so, and he could solemnly assure the emperor that his mother had taken no part in it whatever. Besides, Necker had also done full justice to the emperor in this work.

"Justice, indeed! He calls me the 'necessary man.' The necessary man! and yet, according to his book, the first step necessary to be taken, was to take off this necessary man's head! Yes, I was necessary to repair all that your grandfather had destroyed! It is he who overthrew the monarchy, and brought Louis XVI. to the scaffold!"

"Sire!" exclaimed the young man, deeply agitated, "you are then not aware that my grandfather's estates were confiscated because he defended the king!"

"A fine defence, indeed! If I give a man poison, and then, when he lies in the death-struggle, give him an antidote, can you then maintain that I wished to save this man? It was in this manner that M. Necker defended Louis XVI. The confiscations of which you speak prove nothing. Robespierre's property was also confiscated. Not even Robespierre, Marat, and Danton, have brought such misery upon France as Necker; he it is who made the revolution. You did not see it, but I was present in those days of horror and public distress; but I give you my word that they shall return no more while I live! Your schemers write out their utopias, the simple-minded read these dreams, they are printed and believed in; the common welfare is in everybody's mouth, and soon there is no more bread for the people; it revolts, and that is the usual result of all these fine theories! Your grandfather is to blame for the orgies that brought France to desperation."

Then lowering his voice, from the excited, almost angry tone in which he had been speaking, to a milder one, the emperor approached the young man, who stood before him, pale, and visibly agitated. With that charming air of friendly intimacy that no one knew so well how to assume as Napoleon, he gently pinched the tip of the young man's ear, the emperor's usual way of making peace with any one to whom he wished well, after a little difficulty.

"You are still young," said he; "if you possessed my age and experience, you would judge of these matters differently. Your candor has not offended, but pleased me; I like to see a son defend his mother's cause! Your mother has entrusted you with a very difficult commission, and you have executed it with much spirit. It gives me pleasure to have conversed with you, for I love the young when they are straightforward and not too 'argumentative.' But I can nevertheless give you no false hopes! You will accomplish nothing! If your mother were in prison, I should not hesitate to grant you her release. But she is in exile, and nothing can induce me to recall her."

"But, sire, is one not quite as unhappy far from home and friends, as in prison?"

"Ah, bah! those are romantic notions! You have heard that said about your mother. She is truly greatly to be pitied. With the exception of Paris, she has the whole of Europe for her prison!"

"But, sire, all her friends are in Paris!"

"With her intellect, she will be able to acquire new ones everywhere. Moreover, I cannot understand why she should desire to be in Paris. Why does she so long to place herself in the immediate reach of tyranny? You see I pronounce the decisive word! I am really unable to comprehend it. Can she not go to Rome, Berlin, Vienna, Milan, or London? Yes, London would be the right place! There she can perpetrate libels whenever she pleases. At all of these places I will leave her undisturbed with the greatest pleasure; but Paris is my residence, and there I will tolerate those only who love me! On this the world can depend. I know what would happen, if I should permit your mother to return to Paris. She would commit new follies; she would corrupt those who surround me; she would corrupt Garat, as she once corrupted the tribunal; of course, she would promise all things, but she would, nevertheless, not avoid engaging in politics."

"Sire," I can assure you that my mother does not occupy herself with politics at all; she devotes herself exclusively to the society of her friends, and to literature."

"That is the right word, and I fully understand it. One talks politics while talking of literature, of morals, of the fine arts, and of every conceivable thing! If your mother were in Paris, her latest *bon mots* and phrases would be recited to me daily; perhaps they would be only invented; but I tell you I will have nothing of the kind in the city in which I reside! It would be best for her to go to London; advise her to do so. As far as your grandfather is concerned, I have certainly not said too much; M. Necker had no administrative ability. Once more, inform your mother that I shall never permit her to return to Paris."

"But if sacred interests should require her presence here for a few days, your majesty would at least--"

"What? Sacred interests? What does that mean?"

"Sire," the presence of my mother will be necessary, in order to procure from your majesty's government the return of a sacred debt."

"Ah, bah! sacred! Are not all the debts of the state sacred?"

"Without doubt, sire; but ours is accompanied by peculiar circumstances."

"Peculiar circumstances!" exclaimed the emperor, rising to terminate the long interview, that began to weary him. "What creditor of the state does not say the same of his debt? Moreover, I know too little of your relations toward my government. This matter does not concern me, and I will not be mixed up in it. If the laws are for you, all will go well without my interference; but if it requires influence, I shall have nothing to do with it, for I should be rather against than for you!"

"Sire," said young Staël, venturing to speak once more, as the emperor was on the point of leaving, "sire, my brother and I were anxious to settle in France; but how could we live in a land in which our mother would not be allowed to live with us everywhere?"

Already standing on the threshold of the door, the emperor turned to him hastily. "I have no desire whatever to have you settle here," said he; "on the contrary. I advise you not to do so. Go to England. There they have a *penchant* for Genevese, parlor-politicians, etc.; therefore, go to England; for I must say, I should be rather ill than well disposed toward you[35]!"

[35] Bourrienne, vol. viii., p. 355.

CHAPTER IV
MADAME DE STAËL'S RETURN TO PARIS

Madame de Staël returned to her cherished France with the restoration. She came back thirsting for new honor and renown, and determined, above all, to have her work republished in Germany, its publication having been once suppressed by the imperial police. She entertained the pleasing hope that the new court would forget that she was Necker's daughter, receive her with open arms, and accord her the influence to which her active mind and genius entitled her.

But she was laboring under an error, by which she was not destined to be long deceived. She was received at court with the cold politeness which is more terrible than insult. The king, while speaking of her with his friends, called Madame de Staël "a Chateaubriand in petticoats." The Duchess d'Angoulême seemed never to see the celebrated poetess, and never addressed a word to her; the rest of the court met Madame de Staël armed to the teeth with all the hatred and prejudices of the olden time.

It was also in vain that Madame de Staël endeavored to act an important part at the new court; they refused to regard her as an authority or power, but treated her as a mere authoress; her counsel was ridiculed, and they dared even to question the renown of M. Necker.

"I am unfortunate," said Madame de Staël to Countess Ducayla; "Napoleon hated me because he believed me to possess intellect; these people repel me because I at least possess ordinary human understanding! I can certainly get on very well without them; but, as my presence displeases them, I shall, at least, endeavor to get my money from them."

The "sacred debt" had not been paid under the empire, and it was now Madame de Staël's intention to obtain from the king what the emperor had refused.

She was well aware of the influence which Countess Ducayla exercised over Louis XVIII., and she now hastened to call on the beautiful countess--whose acquaintance she had made under peculiar circumstances, in a romantic love intrigue--in order to renew the friendship they had then vowed to each other.

The countess had not forgotten this friendship, and she was now grateful for the service Madame de Staël had then shown her. She helped to secure the liquidation of the sacred debt, and, upon the order of King Louis, the million was paid over to Madame de Staël. "But," says the countess, in her memoirs, "I believe the recovery of this million cost Madame de Staël four hundred thousand francs, besides a set of jewelry that was worth at least one hundred thousand."

The countess's purse and the jewelry case, however, doubtlessly bore evidence that she might as well have said "I know" as "I believe."

Besides the four hundred thousand francs and the jewelry, Madame de Staël also gave the countess a piece of advice. "Make the most of the favor you now enjoy," said she to her; "but do so quickly, for, as matters are now conducted, I fear that the restoration will soon have to be restored."

"What do you mean by that?" asked the countess, smiling.

"I mean that, with the exception of the king, who perhaps does not say all he thinks, the others are still doing precisely as they always have done, and Heaven knows to what extremities their folly is destined to bring them! They mock at the old soldiers and assist the young priests, and this is the best means of ruining France."

Countess Ducayla considered this prediction of her intellectual friend as a mere cloud with which discontent and disappointed ambition had obscured the otherwise clear vision of Madame de Staël, and ridiculed the idea, little dreaming how soon her words were to be fulfilled.

Madame de Staël consoled herself for her cold reception at court, by receiving the best society of Paris in her parlors, and entertaining them with biting *bon mots* and witty *persiflage*, at the expense of the grand notabilities, who had suddenly arisen with their imposing genealogical trees out of the ruins and oblivion of the past.

Madame de Staël now also remembered the kindness Queen Hortense had shown her during her exile; and not to her only, but also to her friend, Madame Récamier, who had also been exiled by Napoleon, not, however, as his enemies said, "because she was Madame de Staël's friend," but simply because she patronized and belonged to the so-called "little church." The "little church" was an organization born of the spirit of opposition of the Faubourg St. Germain, and a portion of the Catholic clergy, and was one of those things appertaining to the internal relations of France that were most annoying and disagreeable to the emperor.

Queen Hortense had espoused the cause of Madame de Staël and of Madame Récamier with generous warmth. She had eloquently interceded for the recall of both from their exile; and, now that the course of events had restored them to their home, both ladies came to the queen to thank her for her kindness and generosity.

Louise de Cochelet has described this visit of Madame de Staël so wittily, with so much *naïveté*, and with such peculiar local coloring, that we cannot refrain from laying a literal translation of the same before the reader.

CHAPTER V
MADAME DE STAËL'S VISIT
TO QUEEN HORTENSE

Louise de Cochelet relates as follows: "Madame de Staël and Madame Récamier had begged permission of the queen to visit her, for the purpose of tendering their thanks. The queen invited them to visit her at St. Leu, on the following day.

"She asked my advice as to which of the members of her social circle were best qualified to cope with Madame de Staël.

"'I, for my part,' said the queen, 'have not the courage to take the lead in the conversation; one cannot be very intellectual when sad at heart, and I fear my dullness will infect the others.'

"We let quite a number of amiable persons pass before us in review, and I amused myself at the mention of each new name, by saying, 'He is too dull for Madame de Staël.'

"The queen laughed, and the list of those who were to be invited was at last agreed upon. We all awaited the arrival of the two ladies in great suspense. The obligation imposed on us by the queen, of being intellectual at all hazards, had the effect of conjuring up a somewhat embarrassed and stupid expression to our faces. We presented the appearance of actors on the stage looking at each other, while awaiting the rise of the curtain. Jests and *bon mots* followed each other in rapid succession until the arrival of the carriage recalled to our faces an expression of official earnestness.

"Madame Récamier, still young, and very handsome, and with an expression of *naïveté* in her charming countenance, made the impression on me of being a young lady in love, carefully watched over by too severe a *duenna*, her timid, gentle manner contrasted so strongly with the somewhat too masculine self-consciousness of her companion. Madame de Staël is, however, generally admitted to have been good and kind, particularly to this friend, and I only speak of the impression she made on one to whom she was a stranger, at first sight.

"Madame de Staël's extremely dark complexion, her original toilet, her perfectly bare shoulders, of which either might have been very beautiful, but which harmonized very poorly with each other; her whole *ensemble* was far from approximating to the standard of the ideal I had formed of the authoress of Delphine and Corinne. I had almost hoped to find in her one of the heroines she had so beautifully portrayed, and I was therefore struck dumb with astonishment. But, after the first shock, I was at least compelled to acknowledge that she possessed very beautiful and expressive eyes; and yet it seemed impossible for me to find anything in her countenance on which love could fasten, although I have been told that she has often inspired that sentiment.

"When I afterward expressed my astonishment to the queen, she replied: 'It is, perhaps, because she is capable of such great love herself, that she succeeds in inspiring others with love; moreover, it flatters a man's self-love to be noticed by such a woman, and, in the end, one can dispense with beauty, when one has Madame de Staël's intellect.'

"The queen inquired after Madame de Staël's daughter, who had not come with her, and who was said to be truly charming. I believe the young gentlemen of our party could have confronted the beautiful eyes of the daughter with still greater amiability than those of the mother, but an attack of toothache had prevented her coming.

"After the first compliments and salutations, the queen proposed to the ladies to take a look at her park. They seated themselves on the cushions of the queen's large *char à banc*, which has become historic on account of the many high and celebrated personages who have been driven in it at different times. The Emperor Napoleon was, however, not one of this number, as he never visited St. Leu; but, with this exception, there are few of the great and celebrated who have not been seated in it at one time or another.

"As they drove through the park and the forest of Montmorency, in a walk only, the conversation was kept up as in the parlor, and the consumption of intellectuality was continued. The beautiful neighborhood, that reminded one of Switzerland, as it was remarked, was duly admired. Then Italy was spoken of. The queen, who had been somewhat *distraite*, and had good cause to be somewhat sad, and disposed to commune with herself, addressed Madame de Staël with the question, 'You have been in Italy, then?'

"Madame de Staël was, as it were, transfixed with dismay, and the gentlemen exclaimed with one accord: 'And Corinne? and Corinne?'

"'Ah, that is true,' said the queen, in embarrassment, awakening, as it were, from her dreams.

"'Is it possible,' asked M. de Canonville, 'your majesty has not read Corinne?'

"'Yes--no,' said the queen, visibly confused, 'I shall read it again,' and, in order to conceal an emotion that I alone could understand, she abruptly changed the topic of conversation.

"She might have said the truth, and simply informed them that the book had appeared just at the time her eldest son had died in Holland. The king, disquieted at seeing her so profoundly given up to her grief, believed, in accordance with Corvisart's advice, that it was necessary to arouse her from this state of mental dejection at all hazards. It was determined that I should read 'Corinne' to her. She was not in a condition to pay much attention to it, but she had involuntarily retained some remembrance of this romance. Since then, I had several times asked permission of the queen to read Corinne to her, but she had always refused. 'No, no,' said she, 'not yet; this romance has identified itself with my sorrow. Its name alone recalls the most fearful period of my whole life. I have not yet the courage to renew these painful impressions.'

"I, alone, had therefore been able to divine what had embarrassed and moved the queen so much when she replied to the question addressed to her concerning Corinne. But the authoress could, of course, only interpret it as indicating indifference for her master-work, and I told the queen on the following day that it would have been better to have confessed the cause of her confusion to Madame de Staël.

"'Madame de Staël would not have understood me,' said she; 'now, I am lost to her good opinion, she will consider me a simpleton, but it was not the time to speak of myself, and of my painful reminiscences.'

"The large *char à banc* was always preferred to the handsomest carriages (although it was very plain, and consisted of two wooden benches covered with cushions, placed opposite each other), because it was more favorable for conversation. But it afforded no security against inclement weather, and this we were soon to experience. The rain poured in streams, and we all returned to the castle thoroughly wet. A room was there prepared and offered the ladies, in which they might repair the disarrangement of their toilet caused by the storm. I remained with them long, kept there by the questions of Madame de Staël concerning the queen and her son, which questions were fairly showered upon me. There was now no longer a question of intellectuality, but merely of washing, hair-dressing, and reposing, with an entire abandonment of the display of mind, the copiousness of which I had been compelled to admire but a moment before. I said to myself: 'There they are, face to face, like the rest of the world, with material life, these two celebrated women, who are everywhere sought after, and received with such marked consideration. There they are, as wet as myself, and as little poetic.' We were really behind the curtain, but it was shortly to rise again.

"Voices were heard under the window; among other voices, a German accent was audible, and both ladies immediately exclaimed: 'Ah, that is Prince Augustus of Prussia!'

"No one expected the prince, and this meeting with the two ladies had therefore the appearance of being accidental. He had come merely to pay the queen a visit, and it was so near dinner-time, that politeness required that he should be invited to remain. And this was doubtless what he wished.

"The prince had the queen on his right, and Madame de Staël on his left. The servant of the latter had laid a little green twig on her napkin, which she twisted between her fingers while speaking, as was her habit. The conversation was animated, and it was amusing to observe Madame de Staël gesticulating with the little twig in her fingers. One might have supposed that some fairy had given her this talisman, and that her genius was dependent upon this little twig.

"Constantinople, with which city several of the gentlemen were well acquainted, was now the topic of conversation. Madame de Staël thought it would be a delightful task for an intellectual woman, to turn the sultan's head, and then to compel him to give his Turks a constitution. After dinner, freedom of the press was also a topic of conversation.

"Madame de Staël astonished me, not only by the brilliancy of her genius, but also by the deep earnestness with which she treated questions of that kind, for until then custom had not allowed women to discuss such matters. At entertainments, philosophy, morals, sentiment, heroism, and the like, had been the subjects of conversation, but the emperor monopolized politics. His era was that of actions, and, we may say it with pride, of great actions, while the era that followed was essentially that of great words, and of political and literary controversies.

"Madame de Staël spoke to the queen of her motto: 'Do that which is right, happen what may.'

"'In my exile, which you so kindly endeavored to terminate,' said she, 'I often repeated this motto, and thought of you while doing so.'

"While speaking thus, her countenance was illumined by the reflection of inward emotion, and I found her beautiful. She was no longer the woman of mind only, but also the woman of heart and feeling, and I comprehended at this moment how charming she could be.

"Afterward, she had a long conversation with the queen touching the emperor. 'Why was he so angry with me?' asked she. 'He could not have known how much I admired him! I will see him--I shall go to Elba! Do you think he would receive me well? I was born to worship this man, and he has repelled me.'

'Ah, madame,' replied the queen, 'I have often heard the emperor say that he had a great mission to fulfil, and that he could compare his labors with the exertions of a man who, having the summit of a steep mountain ever before his eyes, strains every nerve to attain it, ever toiling painfully upward, and allowing his progress to be arrested by no obstacle whatever. "All the worse for those," said he, "who meet me on my course--I can show them no consideration."'

"'You met him on his course, madame; perhaps he would have extended you a helping hand, after having reached the summit of his mountain.'

"'I must speak with him,' said Madame de Staël; 'I have been injured in his opinion.'

"'I think so too,' replied the queen, 'but you would judge him ill, if you considered him capable of hating any one. He believed you to be his enemy, and he feared you, which was something very unusual for him,' added she, with a smile. 'Now that he is unfortunate, you will show yourself his friend, and prove yourself to be such, and I am satisfied that he will receive you well.'

"Madame de Staël also occupied herself a great deal with the young princes, but she met with worse success with them than with us. It was perhaps in order to judge of their mental capacity, that she showered unsuitable questions upon them.

"'Do you love your uncle?'

"'Very much, madame!'

"'And will you also be as fond of war as he is?'

"'Yes, if it did not cause so much misery.'

'Is it true that he often made you repeat a fable commencing with the words, "The strongest is always in the right?"'

"'Madame, he often made us repeat fables, but this one not oftener than any other.'

"Young Prince Napoleon, a boy of astounding mental capacity and precocious judgment, answered all these questions with the greatest composure, and, at the conclusion of this examination, turned to me and said quite audibly: 'This lady asks a great many questions. Is that what you call being intellectual?'

"After the departure of our distinguished visitors, we all indulged in an expression of opinion concerning them, and young Prince Napoleon was the one upon whom the ladies had made the least flattering impression, but he only ventured to intimate as much in a low voice.

"I for my part had been more dazzled than gladdened by this visit. One could not avoid admiring this genius in spite of its inconsiderateness, and its wanderings, but there was nothing pleasing, nothing graceful and womanly, in Madame de Staël's manner[36]."

[36] Cochelet, Mémoires sur la Reine Hortense, vol. i., pp. 429-440.

CHAPTER VI
THE OLD AND THE NEW ERA

The restoration was accomplished. The allies had at last withdrawn from the kingdom, and Louis XVIII. was now the independent ruler of France. In him, in the returned members of his family, and in the emigrants who were pouring into the country from all quarters, was represented the old era of France, the era of despotic royal power, of brilliant manners, of intrigues, of aristocratic ideas, of ease and luxury. Opposed to them stood the France of the new era, the generation formed by Napoleon and the revolution, the new aristocracy, who possessed no other ancestors than merit and valorous deeds, an aristocracy that had nothing to relate of the *oeil de boeuf* and the *petites maisons*, but an aristocracy that could tell of the battle-field and of the hospitals in which their wounds had been healed.

These two parties stood opposed to each other.

Old and young France now carried on an hourly, continuous warfare at the court of Louis XVIII., with this difference, however, that young France, hitherto ever victorious, now experienced a continuous series of reverses and humiliations. Old France was now victorious. Not victorious through its gallantry and merit, but through its past, which it endeavored to connect with the present, without considering the chasm which lay between.

True, King Louis had agreed, in the treaty of the 11th of April, that none of his subjects should be deprived of their titles and dignities; and the new dukes, princes, marshals, counts, and barons, could therefore appear at court, but they played but a sad and humiliating *rôle*, and they were made to feel that they were only tolerated, and not welcome.

The gentlemen who, before the revolution, had been entitled to seats in the royal equipages, still retained this privilege, but the doors of these equipages were never opened to the gentlemen of the new Napoleonic nobility. "The ladies of the old era still retained their *tabouret*, as well as their grand and little *entrée* to the Tuileries and the Louvre, and it would have been considered very arrogant if the duchesses of the new era had made claim to similar honors."

It was the Duchess d'Angoulême who took the lead and set the Faubourg St. Germain an example of intolerance and arrogant pretensions in ignoring the empire. She was the most unrelenting enemy of the new era, born of the revolution, and of its representatives; it is true, however, that she, who was the daughter of the beheaded royal pair, and who had herself so long languished in the Temple, had been familiar with the horrors of the revolution in their saddest and most painful features. She now determined, as she could no longer punish, to at least forget this era, and to seem to be entirely oblivious of its existence.

At one of the first dinners given by the king to the allies, the Duchess d'Angoulême, who sat next to the King of Bavaria, pointed to the Grand-duke of Baden, and asked: "Is not this the prince who married a princess of Bonaparte's making? What weakness to ally one's self in such a manner with that general!"

The duchess did not or would not remember that the King of Bavaria, as well as the Emperor of Austria, who sat on her other side, and could well hear her words, had also allied themselves with General Bonaparte.

After she had again installed herself in the rooms she had formerly occupied in the Tuileries, the duchess asked old Dubois, who had formerly tuned her piano, and had retained this office under the empire, and who now showed her the new and elegant instruments provided by Josephine-- she asked him: "What has become of my piano?"

This "piano" had been an old and worn-out concern, and the duchess was surprised at not finding it, as though almost thirty years had not passed since she had seen it last; as though the 10th of August, 1792, the day on which the populace demolished the Tuileries, had never been!

But the period from 1795 to 1814 was ignored on principle, and the Bourbons seemed really to have quite forgotten that more than one night lay between the last levee of King Louis XVI. and the levee of to-day of King Louis XVIII. They seemed astonished that persons they had known as children had grown up since they last saw them, and insisted on treating every one as they had done in 1789.

After the Empress Josephine's death, Count d'Artois paid a visit to Malmaison, a place that had hardly existed before the revolution, and which owed its creation to Josephine's love and taste for art.

The empress, who had a great fondness for botany, had caused magnificent greenhouses to be erected at Malmaison; in these all the plants and flowers of the world had been collected. Knowing her taste, all the princes of Europe had sent her, in the days of her grandeur, in order to afford her a moment's gratification, the rarest exotics. The Prince Regent of England had even found means, during the war with France, to send her a number of rare West-Indian plants. In this manner her collection had become the richest and most complete in all Europe.

Count d'Artois, as above said, had come to Malmaison to view this celebrated place of sojourn of Josephine, and, while being conducted through the greenhouses, he exclaimed, as though he recognized his old flowers of 1789: "Ah, here are our plants of Trianon!"

And, like their masters the Bourbons, the emigrants had also returned to France with the same ideas with which they had fled the country. They endeavored, in all their manners, habits, and pretensions, to begin again precisely where they had left off in 1789. They had so lively an appreciation of their own merit, that they took no notice whatever of other people's, and yet their greatest merit consisted in having emigrated.

For this merit they now demanded a reward.

All of these returned emigrants demanded rewards, positions, and pensions, and considered it incomprehensible that those who were already in possession were not at once deprived of them. Intrigues were the order of the day, and in general the representatives of the old era succeeded in supplanting those of the new era in offices and pensions as well as in court honors. All the high positions in the army were filled by the marquises, dukes, and counts, of the old era, who had sewed tapestry and picked silk in Coblentz, while the France of the new era was fighting on the battle-field, and they now began to teach the soldiers of the empire the old drill of 1780.

The etiquette of the olden time was restored, and the same luxurious and lascivious disposition prevailed among these cavaliers of the former century which had been approved in the *oeil de boeuf* and in the *petites maisons* of the old era.

These old cavaliers felt contempt for the young Frenchmen of the new era on account of their pedantic morality; they scornfully regarded men who perhaps had not more than one mistress, and to whom the wife of a friend was so sacred, that they never dared to approach her with a disrespectful thought even.

These legitimist gentlemen entertained themselves chiefly with reflections over the past, and their own grandeur. In the midst of the many new things by which they were surrounded, some of which they unfortunately found it impossible to ignore, it was their sweetest relaxation to give themselves up entirely to the remembrance of the old *régime*, and when they spoke of this era, they forgot their age and debility, and were once more the young *roués* of the *oeil de boeuf.*

Once in the antechamber of King Louis XVIII., while the Marquis de Chimène and the Duke de Lauraguais, two old heroes of the frivolous era, in which the boudoir and the *petites maisons* were the battle-field, and the myrtle instead of the laurel the reward of victory, while these gentlemen were conversing of some occurrence under the old government, the Duke de Lauraguais, in order to more nearly fix the date of the occurrence of which they were speaking, remarked to the marquis, "It was in the year in which I had my *liaison* with your wife."

"Ah, yes," replied the marquis, with perfect composure, "that was in the year 1776."

Neither of the gentlemen found anything strange in this allusion to the past. The *liaison* in question had been a perfectly commonplace matter, and it would have been as ridiculous in the duke to deny it as for the marquis to have shown any indignation.

The wisest and most enlightened of all these gentlemen was their head, King Louis XVIII. himself.

He was well aware of the errors of those who surrounded him, and placed but little confidence in the representatives of the old court. But he was nevertheless powerless to withdraw himself from their influence, and after he had accorded the people the charter, in opposition to the will and opinion of the whole royal family, of his whole court and of his ministers, and had sworn to support it in spite of the opposition of "Monsieur" and the Prince de Condé, who was in the habit of calling the charter "*Mademoiselle la Constitution de 1791,*" Louis withdrew to the retirement of his apartments in the Tuileries, and left his minister Blacas to attend to the little details of government, the king deeming the great ones only worthy of his attention.

CHAPTER VII
KING LOUIS XVIII

King Louis XVIII. was, however, in the retirement of his palace, still the most enlightened and unprejudiced of the representatives of the old era; he clearly saw many things to which his advisers purposely closed their eyes. To his astonishment, he observed that the men who had risen to greatness under Bonaparte, and who had fallen to the king along with the rest of his inheritance, were not so ridiculous, awkward, and foolish, as they had been represented to be.

"I had been made to suppose," said Louis XVIII., "that these generals of Bonaparte were peasants and ruffians, but such is not the case. He schooled these men well. They are polite, and quite as shrewd as the representatives of the old court. We must conduct ourselves very cautiously toward them."

This kind of recognition of the past which sometimes escaped Louis XVIII., was a subject of bitter displeasure to the gentlemen of the old era, and they let the king perceive it.

King Louis felt this, and, in order to conciliate his court, he often saw himself compelled to humiliate "the *parvenus*" who had forced themselves among the former.

Incessant quarrelling and intriguing within the Tuileries was the consequence, and Louis was often dejected, uneasy, and angry, in the midst of the splendor that surrounded him.

"I am angry with myself and the others," said he on one occasion to an intimate friend. "An invisible and secret power is ever working in opposition to my will, frustrating my plans, and paralyzing my authority."

"And yet you are king!"

"Undoubtedly I am king!" exclaimed Louis, angrily; "but am I also master? The king is he who all his life long receives ambassadors, gives tiresome audiences, listens to annihilating discourses, goes in state to Notre-Dame, dines in public once a year, and is pompously buried in St. Denis when he dies. The master is he who commands and can enforce obedience, who puts an end to intriguing, and can silence old women as well as priests.

Bonaparte was king and master at the same time! His ministers were his clerks, the kings his brothers merely his agents, and his courtiers nothing more than his servants. His ministers vied with his senate in servility, and his *Corps Législatif* sought to outdo his senate and the church in subserviency. He was an extraordinary and an enviable man, for he had not only devoted servants and faithful friends, but also an accommodating church[37]."

[37] Mémoires d'une Femme de Qualité, vol. v., p. 35.

King Louis XVIII., weary of the incessant intrigues with which his courtiers occupied themselves, withdrew himself more and more into the retirement of his palace, and left the affairs of state to the care of M. de Blacas, who, with all his arrogance and egotism, knew very little about governing.

The king preferred to entertain himself with his friends, to read them portions of his memoirs, to afford them an opportunity of admiring his verses, and to regale them with his witty and not always chaste anecdotes; he preferred all these things to tedious and useless disputes with his ministers. He had given his people the charter, and his ministers might now govern in accordance with this instrument.

"The people demand liberty," said the king. "I give them enough of it to protect them against despotism, without according them unbridled license. Formerly, the taxes appointed by my mere will would have made me odious; now the people tax themselves. Hereafter, I have nothing to do but to confer benefits and show mercy, for the responsibility for all the evil that is done will rest entirely with my ministers[38]."

[38] Mémoires d'une Femme de Qualité, vol. i., p. 410.

While his ministers were thus governing according to the charter, and "doing evil," the king, who now had nothing but "good" to do, was busying himself in settling the weighty questions of the old etiquette.

One of the most important features of this etiquette was the question of the fashions that should now be introduced at court; for it was, of course, absurd to think of adopting the fashions of the empire, and thereby recognize at court that there had really been a change since 1789.

They desired to effect a counter-revolution, not only in politics, but also in fashions; and this important matter occupied the attention of the grand dignitaries of the court for weeks before the first grand levee that the king was to hold in the Tuilerics. But, as nothing was accomplished by their united wisdom, the king finally held a private consultation with his most intimate gentleman and lady friends on this important matter, that had, unfortunately, not been determined by the charter.

The grand-master of ceremonies, M. de Bregé, declared to the king that it was altogether improper to continue the fashions of the empire at the court of the legitimate King of France.

"We are, therefore, to have powder, coats-of-mail, etc.," observed the king.

M. de Bregé replied, with all gravity, that he had given this subject his earnest consideration day and night, but that he had not yet arrived at a conclusion worthy of the grand-master of ceremonies of the legitimate king.

"Sire," said the Duke de Chartres, smiling, "I, for my part, demand knee-breeches, shoe-buckles, and the cue."

"But I," exclaimed the Prince de Poir, who had remained in France during the empire, "I demand damages, if we are to be compelled to return to the old fashions and clothing before the new ones are worn out!"

The grand-master of ceremonies replied to this jest at his expense with a profound sigh only; and the king at last put an end to this great question, by deciding that every one should be permitted to follow the old or new fashions, according to his individual taste and inclination.

The grand-master of ceremonies was compelled to submit to this royal decision; but in doing so he observed, with profound sadness: "Your majesty is pleased to smile, but dress makes half the man; uniformity of attire confounds the distinctions of rank, and leads directly to an agrarian law."

"Yes, marquis," exclaimed the king, "you think precisely as Figaro. Many a man laughs at a judge in a short dress, who trembles before a procurator in a long gown[39]."

[39] Mémoires d'une Femme de Qualité, vol. i., p. 384.

But while the king suppressed the counter-revolution in fashions, he allowed the grand-master of ceremonies to reintroduce the entire etiquette of the old era. In conformity with this etiquette, the king could not rise from his couch in the morning until the doors had been opened to all those who had the *grande entrée*--that is to say, to the officers of his household, the marshals of France, several favored ladies; further, to his *cafetier*, his tailor, the bearer of his slippers, his barber, with two assistants, his watchmaker, and his apothecaries.

The king was dressed in the presence of all these favored individuals, etiquette permitting him only to adjust his necktie himself, but requiring him, however, to empty his pockets of their contents of the previous day.

The usage of the old era, "the public dinner of the royal family," was also reintroduced; and the grand-master of ceremonies not only found it necessary to make preparations for this dinner weeks beforehand, but the king was also compelled to occupy himself with this matter, and to appoint for this great ceremony the necessary "officers of provisions"--that is to say, the wine-taster, the cup-bearers, the grand doorkeepers, and the cook-in-chief.

At this first grand public dinner, the celebrated and indispensable "ship" of the royal board stood again immediately in front of the king's seat. This old "ship" of the royal board, an antique work of art which the city of Paris had once presented to a King of France, had also been lost in the grand shipwreck of 1792, and the grand-master of ceremonies had been compelled to have a new one made by the court jeweller for the occasion. This "ship" was a work in gilded silver, in form of a vessel deprived of its masts and rigging; and in the same, between two golden plates, were contained the perfumed napkins of the king. In accordance with the old etiquette, no one, not even the princes and princesses, could pass the "ship" without making a profound obeisance, which they were also compelled to make on passing the royal couch.

The king restored yet another fashion of the old era--the fashion of the "royal lady-friends."

Like his brother the Count d'Artois, Louis XVIII. also had his lady-friends; and among these the beautiful and witty Countess Ducayla occupied the first position. It was her office to amuse the king, and dissipate the dark clouds that were only too often to be seen on the brow of King Louis, who was chained to his arm-chair by ill-health, weakness, and excessive corpulency. She narrated to him the *chronique scandaleuse* of the imperial court; she reminded him of the old affairs of his youth, which the king knew how to relate with so much wit and humor, and which he so loved to relate; it devolved upon her to examine the letters of the "black cabinet," and to read the more interesting ones to the king.

King Louis was not ungrateful to his royal friend, and he rewarded her in a truly royal manner for sometimes banishing *ennui* from his apartments. Finding that the countess had no intimate acquaintance with the contents of the Bible, he gave her the splendid Bible of Royaumont, ornamented with one hundred and fifty magnificent engravings, after paintings of Raphael. Instead of tissue-paper, a thousand-franc note covered each of these engravings[40].

[40] Amours et Galanteries des Rois de France, par St. Edme, vol. ii., p. 383. Mémoires d'une Femme de Qualité, vol. i., p. 409.

On another occasion, the king gave her a copy of the "Charter;" and in this each leaf was also covered with a thousand-franc note, as in the Bible.

For so many proofs of the royal generosity, the beautiful countess, perhaps willingly, submitted to be called "the royal snuff-box," which appellation had its origin in the habit which the king fondly indulged in of strewing snuff on the countess's lovely shoulder, and then snuffing it up with his nose.

CHAPTER VIII
THE DRAWING-KOOM OF THE
DUCHESS OF ST. LEU

While the etiquette and frivolity of the old era were being introduced anew at the Tuileries, and while M. de Blacas was governing in complacent recklessness, time was progressing, notwithstanding his endeavors to turn it backward in his flight.

While, out of the incessant conflict between the old and the new France, a discontented France was being born, Napoleon, the Emperor of Elba, was forming great plans of conquest, and preparing in secret understanding with the faithful, to leave his place of exile and return to France.

He well knew that he could rely on his old army--on the army who loudly cried, *"Vive le roi!"* and then added, *sotto voce, "de Rome, et son petit papa* [41]!"

[41] Cochelet, Mémoires sur la Reine Hortense, vol. iii, p. 121.

Hortense, the new Duchess of St. Leu, took but little part in all these things. She had, notwithstanding her youth and beauty, in a measure taken leave of the world. She felt herself to be no longer the woman, but only the mother; her sons were the objects of all her tenderness and love, and she lived for them only. In her retirement at St. Leu, her time was devoted to the arts, to reading, and to study; and, after having been thus occupied throughout the day, she passed the evening in her drawing-room, in unrestrained intellectual conversation with her friends.

For she had friends who had remained true, notwithstanding the obscurity into which she had withdrawn herself, and who, although they filled important positions at the new court, had retained their friendship for the solitary dethroned queen.

With these friends the Duchess of St. Leu conversed, in the evening, in her parlor, of the grand and beautiful past, giving themselves up entirely to these recollections, little dreaming that this harmless relaxation could awaken suspicion.

For the Duke of Otranto, who had succeeded in his shrewdness in retaining his position of minister of police, as well under Louis XVIII. as under Napoleon, had his spies everywhere; he knew of all that was said in every parlor of Paris; he knew also that it was the custom, in the parlors of the Duchess of St. Leu, to look from the dark present back at the brilliant past, and to console one's self for the littleness of the present, with the recollection of the grandeur of departed days! And Fouché, or rather the Duke of Otranto, knew how to utilize everything.

In order to arouse Minister Blacas out of his stupid dream of security, to a realizing sense of the grave events that were taking place, Fouché told him that a conspiracy against the government was being formed in the parlors of the Duchess of St. Leu; that all those who were secret adherents of Bonaparte were in the habit of assembling there, and planning the deliverance of the emperor from Elba. In order, however, on the other hand, to provide against the possibility of Napoleon's return, the Duke of Otranto hastened to the Duchess of St. Leu, to warn her and conjure her to be on her guard against the spies by whom she was surrounded, as suspicion might be easily excited against her at court.

Hortense paid no attention to this warning; she considered precaution unnecessary, and was not willing to deprive herself of her one happiness- -that of seeing her friends, and of conversing with them in a free and unconstrained manner.

The parlors of the duchess, therefore, continued to be thrown open to her faithful friends, who had also been the faithful servants of the emperor; and the Dukes of Bassano, of Friaul, of Ragusa, of the Moskwa, and their wives, as well as the gallant Charles de Labedoyère, and the acute Count Renault de Saint-Jean d'Angely, still continued to meet in the parlors of the Duchess of St. Leu.

The voice of hostility was raised against them with ever-increasing hostility; the reunions that took place at St. Leu were day by day portrayed at the Tuileries in more hateful colors; and the poor duchess, who lived in sorrow and retirement in her apartments, became an object of hatred and envy to these proud ladies of the old aristocracy, who were unable to comprehend how this woman could be thought of while they were near, although she had been the ornament of the imperial court, and who was considered amiable, intellectual, and beautiful, even under the legitimate dynasty.

Hortense heard of the ridiculous and malicious reports which had been circulated concerning her, and, for the sake of her friends and sons, she resolved to put an end to them.

"I must leave my dear St. Leu and go to Paris," said she. "There they can better observe all my actions. Reason demands that I should conform myself to circumstances."

She therefore abandoned her quiet home at St. Leu, and repaired with her children and her court to Paris, to again take up her abode in her dwelling in the Rue de la Victoire.

But this step gave fresh fuel to the calumnies of her enemies, who saw in her the embodied remembrance of the empire which they hated and at the same time feared.

The Bonapartists still continued their visits to her parlors, as before; and no appeals, no representations could induce Hortense to close her doors against her faithful friends, for fear that their fidelity might excite suspicion against herself.

In order, however, to contradict the report that adherents of Napoleon only were in the habit of frequenting her parlors, the duchess also extended the hospitalities of her parlors to the strangers who brought letters of recommendation, and who desired to be introduced to her. Great numbers hastened to avail themselves of this permission.

The most brilliant and select circle was soon assembled around the duchess. There, were to be found the great men of the empire, who came out of attachment; distinguished strangers, who came out of admiration; and, finally, the aristocrats of the old era, who came out of curiosity, who came to see if the Duchess of St. Leu was really so intelligent, amiable, and graceful, as she was said to be.

The parlors of the duchess were therefore more talked of in Paris than they had been at St. Leu. The old duchesses and princesses of the Faubourg St. Germain, with all their ancestors, prejudices, and pretensions, were enraged at hearing this everlasting praise of the charming queen, and endeavored to appease their wrath by renewed hostilities against its object.

It was not enough that she was calumniated, at court and in society, as a dangerous person; the arm of the press was also wielded against her.

As we have said, Hortense was the embodied remembrance of the empire, and it was therefore determined that she should be destroyed. *Brochures* and pamphlets were published, in which the king was appealed to, to banish from Paris, and even from France, the dangerous woman who was conspiring publicly, and even under the very eyes of the government, for Napoleon, and to banish with her the two children also, the two Napoleons; "for," said these odious accusers, "to leave these two princes here, means to raise in France wolves that would one day ravage their country[42]."

[42] Cochelet, Mémoires sur la Reins Hortense, vol. ii., p. 330.

Hortense paid but little attention to these reports and calumnies. She was too much accustomed to being misunderstood and wrongly judged, to allow herself to be disquieted thereby. She knew that calumnies were never refuted by contradiction, and that it was therefore better to meet them with proud silence, and to conquer them by contempt, instead of giving them new life by combating and contradicting them.

She herself entertained such contempt for calumny that she never allowed anything abusive to be said in her presence that would injure any one in her estimation. When, on one occasion, while she was still Queen of Holland, a lady of Holland took occasion to speak ill of another lady, on account of her political opinions, the queen interrupted her, and said: "Madame, here I am a stranger to all parties, and receive all persons with the same consideration, for I love to hear every one well spoken of; and I generally receive an unfavorable impression of those only who speak ill of others[43]."

[43] Cochelet, vol. i., p. 378.

And, strange to say, she herself was ever the object of calumny and accusation.

"During twenty-five years, I have never been separated from Princess Hortense," says Louise de Cochelet, "and I have never observed in her the slightest feeling of bitterness against any one; ever good and gentle, she never failed to take an interest in those who were unhappy; and she endeavored to help them whenever and wherever they presented themselves. And this noble and gentle woman was always the object of hatred and absurd calumnies, and against all this she was armed with the integrity and purity of her actions and intentions only[44]."

[44] Cochelet, vol. i., p. 378.

Nor did Hortense now think of contradicting the calumnies that had been circulated concerning her. Her mind was occupied with other and far more important matters.

An ambassador of her husband, who resided in Florence, had come to Paris in order to demand of Hortense, in the name of Louis Bonaparte, his two sons.

After much discussion, he had finally declared that he would be satisfied, if his wife would send him his eldest son, Napoleon Louis, only.

But the loving mother could not and would not consent to a separation from either of her children; and as, in spite of her entreaties, her husband persisted in refusing to allow her to retain both of them, she resolved, in the anguish of maternal love, to resort to the most extreme means to retain the possession of her sons.

She informed her husband's ambassador that it was her fixed purpose to retain possession of her children, and appealed to the law to recognize and protect them, and not allow her sons to be deprived of their rights as Frenchmen, by going into a compulsory exile.

While the Duchess of St. Leu was being accused of conspiring in favor of Napoleon, her whole soul was occupied with the one question, which was to decide whether one of her sons could be torn from her side or not; and, if she conspired at all, it was only with her lawyer in order to frustrate her husband's plans.

But the calumnies and accusations of the press were nevertheless continued; and at last her friends thought it necessary to lay before the queen a journal that contained a violent and abusive article against her, and to request that they might be permitted to reply to it.

"With a sad smile, Hortense read the article and returned the newspaper.

"It is extremely mortifying to be scorned by one's countrymen," said she, "but it would be useless to make any reply. I can afford to disregard such attacks--they are powerless to harm me."

But when on the following morning the same journal contained a venomous and odious article levelled at her husband, Louis Bonaparte, her generous indignation was aroused, and, oblivious of all their disagreements, and even of the process now pending between them, she remembered only that it was the father of her children whom they had dared to attack, and that he was not present to defend himself. It therefore devolved upon her to defend him.

"I am enraged, and I desire that M. Després shall reply to this article at once," said Hortense. "Although paternal love on the one side, and maternal love on the other, has involved us in a painful process, it nevertheless concerns no one else, and it disgraces neither of us. I should be in despair, if this sad controversy were made the pretext for insulting the father of my children and the honored name he bears. For the very reason that I stand alone, am I called on to defend the absent to the best of my ability. Therefore let M. Després come to me; I will instruct him how to answer this disgraceful article!"

On the following day, an able and eloquent article in defence of Louis Bonaparte appeared in the journal--an article that shamed and silenced his accusers--an article which the prince, whose cause it so warmly espoused, probably never thought of attributing to the wife to whose maternal heart be had caused such anguish[45].

[45] Cochelet, vol. i., p. 303.

CHAPTER IX
THE BURIAL OF LOUIS XVI. AND HIS WIFE

The earnest endeavors of the Bourbon court to find the resting-place of the remains of the royal couple who had died on the scaffold, and who had expiated the crimes of their predecessors rather than their own, were at last successful. The remains of the illustrious martyrs had been sought for in accordance with the directions of persons who had witnessed their sorrowful and contemptuous burial, and the body of Louis XVI. was found in a desolate corner of the grave-yard of St. Roch, and in another place also that of Queen Marie Antoinette.

It was the king's wish, and a perfectly natural and just one, to inter these bodies in the royal vault at St. Denis, but he wished to do it quietly and without pomp; his acute political tact taught him that these sad remains should not be made the occasion of a political demonstration, and that it was unwise to permit the bones of Louis XVI. to become a new apple of discord.

But the king's court, even his nearest relatives, his ministers, and the whole troop of arrogant courtiers, who desired, by means of an ostentatious interment, not only to show a proper respect for the beheaded royal pair, but also to punish those whom they covertly called "regicides," and whom they were nevertheless now compelled to tolerate--the king's entire court demanded a solemn and ceremonious interment; and Louis, who, as he himself had said, "was king, but not master," was compelled to yield to this demand.

Preparations were therefore made for an ostentatious interment of the royal remains, and it was determined that the melancholy rites should take place on the 21st of January, 1815, the anniversary of painful memories and unending regret for the royal family.

M. de Chateaubriand, the noble and intelligent eulogist and friend of the Bourbons, caused an article to be inserted in the *Journal des Débats*, in which he announced the impending ceremony. This article was then republished in pamphlet form; and so great was the sympathy of the Parisians in the approaching event, that thirty thousand copies were disposed of, in Paris alone, in one day.

On the 20th of January the graves of the martyrs were opened, and all the princes of the royal house who were present, knelt down at the edge of the grave to mingle their prayers with those of the thousands who had accompanied them to the church-yard.

But the king was right. This act, that appeared to some to be a mere act of justice, seemed an insult to others, and reminded them of the dark days of error and fanaticism, in which they had allowed themselves to be drawn into the vortex of the general delirium. Many of those who in the Assembly had voted for the death of the king, were now residing at Paris, and even at court, as for instance Fouché, and to them the approaching ceremony seemed an insult.

"Are you aware," exclaimed Descourtis, as he rushed into the apartment of Cambacérès, who was at that moment conversing with the Count de Pere, "have you already been informed that this ceremony is really to take place to-morrow?"

"Yes, to-morrow is the fated day. To-morrow we are to be delivered over to the daggers of fanatics."

"Is this the pardon that was promised us?"

"As for that," exclaimed the Count de Pere (a good royalist), "I was not aware that there was an article in the constitution forbidding the reinterment of the mortal remains of the royal pair. The proceeding will be perfectly lawful."

"It is their purpose to infuriate the populace," exclaimed Descourtis, pale with inward agitation. "Old recollections are to be recalled and a mute accusation hurled at us. But we shall some day be restored to power again, and then we will remember also!"

Cambacérès, who had listened to this conversation in silence, now stepped forward, and, taking Descourtis's hand in his own, pressed it tenderly.

"Ah, my friend," said he, in sad and solemn tones, "I would we were permitted to march behind the funeral-car in mourning-robes to-morrow! We owe this proof of repentance to France and to ourselves!"

The solemn funeral celebration took place on the following day. All Paris took part in it. Every one, even the old republicans, the Bonapartists as well as the royalists, joined the funeral procession, in order to testify that they had abandoned the past and were repentant.

Slowly and solemnly, amid the ringing of all the bells, the roll of the drum, the thunders of artillery, and the chants of the clergy, the procession moved onward.

The golden crown, which hung suspended over the funeral-car, shone lustrously in the sunlight. It had fallen from the heads of the royal pair while they still lived; it now adorned them in death.

Slowly and solemnly the procession moved onward; it had arrived at the Boulevards which separates the two streets of Montmartre. Suddenly a terrible, thousand-voiced cry of horror burst upon the air.

The crown, which hung suspended over the funeral-car, had fallen down, touching the coffins with a dismal sound, and then broke into fragments on the glittering snow of the street.

This occurred on the 21st of January; two months later, at the same hour, and on the same day, the crown of Louis XVIII. fell from his head, and Napoleon placed it on his own!

CHAPTER X
NAPOLEON'S RETURN FROM ELBA

A cry of tremendous import reverberated through Paris, all France, and all Europe, in the first days of March, 1815. Napoleon, it was said, had quitted Elba, and would soon arrive in France!

The royalists heard it with dismay, the Bonapartists with a delight that they hardly took the pains to conceal.

Hortense alone took no part in the universal delight of the imperialists. Her soul was filled with profound sadness and dark forebodings. "I lament this step," said she; "I would have sacrificed every thing to prevent his return to France, because I am of the belief that no good can come of it. Many will declare for, and many against him, and we shall have a civil war, of which the emperor himself may be the victim[46]."

[46] Cochelet, vol. ii., p. 348.

In the meanwhile the general excitement was continually increasing; it took possession of every one, and at this time none would have been capable of giving cool and sensible advice.

Great numbers of the emperor's friends came to the Duchess of St. Leu, and demanded of her counsel, assistance, and encouragement, accusing her of indifference and want of sympathy, because she did not share their hopes, and was sad instead of rejoicing with them.

But the spies of the still ruling government, who lay in wait around the queen's dwelling, did not hear her words; they only saw that the emperor's former generals and advisers were in the habit of repairing to her parlors, and that was sufficient to stamp Hortense as the head of the conspiracy which had for its object the return of Napoleon to France.

The queen perceived the danger of her situation, but she bowed her head to receive the blows of Fate in silent resignation. "I am environed by torments and perplexities," said she, "but I see no means of avoiding them. There is no resource for me but to arm myself with courage, and that I will do."

The royal government, however, still hoped to be able to stem the advancing tide, and compel the waves of insurrection to surge backward and destroy those who had set them in motion.

They proposed to treat the great event which made France glow with new pulsations, as a mere insurrection, that had been discovered in good time, and could therefore be easily repressed. They therefore determined, above all, to seize and render harmless the "conspirators," that is to say, all those of whom it was known that they had remained faithful to the emperor in their hearts.

Spies surrounded the houses of all the generals, dukes, and princes of the empire, and it was only in disguise and by the greatest dexterity that they could evade the vigilance of the police.

The Duchess of St. Leu was at last also compelled to yield to the urgent entreaties of her friends, and seek an asylum during these days of uncertainty and danger. She quitted her dwelling in disguise, and, penetrating through the army of spies who lay in wait around the house and in the street in which she resided, she happily succeeded in reaching the hiding-place prepared for her by a faithful servant of her mother. She had already confided her children to another servant who had remained true to her in her time of trouble.

The Duke of Otranto, now once more the faithful Fouché of the empire, was also to have been arrested, but he managed to effect his escape. General Lavalette--who was aware that the dwelling of the Duchess of St. Leu was no longer watched by the police, who had discovered that the duchess was no longer there--Lavalette took advantage of this circumstance, and concealed himself in her dwelling, and M. de Dandré, the chief of police, who had vainly endeavored to catch the so-called conspirators, exclaimed in anguish: "It is impossible to find any one; it has been so much noised about that these Bonapartists were to be arrested, that they are now all hidden away."

Like a bombshell the news suddenly burst upon the anxious and doubting capital: "The emperor has been received by the people in Grenoble with exultation, and the troops that were to have been led against him have, together with their chieftain, Charles de Labedoyère, gone over to the emperor. The gates of the city were thrown open, and the people advanced to meet him with shouts of welcome and applause; and now Napoleon stood no longer at the head of a little body of troops, but at the head of a small army that was increasing with every hour."

The government still endeavored, through its officials and through the public press, to make the Parisians disbelieve this intelligence.

But the government had lost faith in itself. It heard the old, the hated cry, "Vive l'empereur!" resounding through the air; it heard the fluttering of the victorious battle-flags of Marengo, Arcola, Jena, and Austerlitz! The Emperor Napoleon was still the conquering hero, who swayed destiny and compelled it to declare for him.

A perfect frenzy of dismay took possession of the royalists; and when they learned that Napoleon had already arrived in Lyons, that its inhabitants had received him with enthusiasm, and that its garrison had also declared for him, their panic knew no bounds.

The royalist leaders assembled at the house of Count de la Pere, for the purpose of holding a last great discussion and consultation. The most eminent persons, men and women, differing widely on other subjects, but a unit on this point, assembled here with the same feelings of patriotic horror, and with the same desire to promote the general welfare. There were Madame de Staël, Benjamin Constant, Count Lainé, and Chateaubriand; there were the Duke de Némours, and Count de la Pere, and around them gathered the whole troop of anxious royalists, expecting and hoping that the eloquent lips of these celebrated personages who stood in their midst would give them consolation and new life.

Benjamin Constant spoke first. He said that, to Napoleon, that is, to force, force must be opposed. Bonaparte was armed with the love of the soldiers, they must arm themselves with the love of the citizens. His appearance was imposing, like the visage of Caesar; it would be necessary to oppose to him an equally sublime countenance. Lafayette should, therefore, be made commander-in-chief of the French army.

M. de Chateaubriand exclaimed, with noble indignation, that the first step to be taken by the government was to punish severely a ministry that was so short-sighted, and had committed so many faults. Lainé declared, with a voice tremulous with emotion, that all was lost, and that but one means of confounding tyranny remained; a scene, portraying the whole terror, dismay and grief of the capital at the approach of the hated enemy, should be arranged. In accordance with this plan, the whole population of Paris--the entire National Guard, the mothers, the young girls, the children, the old and the young--were to pass out of the city, and await the tyrant; and this aspect of a million of men fleeing from the face of a single human being was to move or terrify him who came to rob them of their peace!

In her enthusiastic and energetic manner, Madame de Staël pronounced an anathema against the usurper who was about to kindle anew, in weeping, shivering France, the flames of war.

All were touched, enthusiastic, and agitated, but they could do nothing but utter fine phrases; and all that fell from the eloquent lips of these celebrated poets and politicians was, as it were, nothing more than a bulletin concerning the condition of the patient, and concerning the mortal wounds which he had received. This patient was France; and the royalists, who were assembled in the house of Count de la Pere, now felt that the patient's case was hopeless, and that nothing remained to them but to go into exile, and bemoan his sad fate[47]!

[47] Mémoires d'une Femme de Qualité, vol. i., p. 99.

CHAPTER XI
LOUIS XVIII.'S DEPARTURE AND NAPOLEON'S ARRIVAL

While the royalists were thus considering, hesitating, and despairing, King Louis XVIII. had alone retained his composure and sense of security. That is to say, they had taken care not to inform him of the real state of affairs. On the contrary, he had been informed that Bonaparte had been everywhere received with coldness and silence, and that the army would not respond to his appeal, but would remain true to the king. The exultation with which the people everywhere received the advancing emperor found, therefore, no echo in the Tuileries, and the crowd who pressed around the king when he repaired to the hall of the *Corps Législatif* to hold an encouraging address, was not the people, but the royalists--those otherwise so haughty ladies and gentlemen of the old nobility, who again, as on the day of the first entrance, acted the part to which the people were not disposed to adapt themselves, and transformed themselves for a moment into the people, in order to show to the king the demonstrations of his people's love.

The king was completely deceived. M. de Blacas told the king of continuous reverses to Napoleon's arms, while the emperor's advance was in reality a continuous triumph. They had carried this deception so far that they had informed the king that Lyons had closed its gates to Napoleon, and that Ney was advancing to meet him, vowing that he would bring the emperor back to Paris in an iron cage.

The king was therefore composed, self-possessed, and resolute, when suddenly his brother, the Count d'Artois, and the Duke of Orleans, who, according to the king's belief, occupied Lyons as a victor, arrived in Paris alone, as fugitives, abandoned by their soldiers and servants, and informed Louis that Lyons had received the emperor with open arms, and that no resource had been left them but to betake themselves to flight.

And a second, and still more terrible, item of intelligence followed the first. Ney, the king's hope, the last support of his tottering throne, Ney had not had the heart to maintain a hostile position toward his old companion in arms. Ney had gone over to the emperor, and his army had followed him with exultation.

The king's eyes were now opened, he now saw the truth, and learned how greatly he had been deceived.

"Alas," cried he, sadly, "Bonaparte fell because he would not listen to the truth, and I shall fall because they would not tell me the truth!"

At this moment, and while the king was eloquently appealing to his brothers and relatives, and to the gentlemen of his court who surrounded him, to tell him the whole truth, the door opened, and the Minister Blacas, until then so complacent, so confident of victory, now stepped in pale and trembling.

The truth, which he had so long concealed from the king, was now plainly impressed on his pale, terrified countenance. The king had desired to hear the truth; it stood before him in his trembling minister.

A short interval of profound silence occurred; the eyes of all were fastened on the count, and, in the midst of the general silence, he was heard to say, in a voice choked with emotion: "Sire, all is lost; the army, as well as the people, betray your majesty. It will be necessary for your majesty to leave Paris."

The king staggered backward for an instant, and then fastened an inquiring glance on the faces of all who were present. No one dared to return his gaze with a glance of hope. They all looked down sorrowfully.

The king understood this mute reply, and a deep sigh escaped his breast.

"The tree bears its fruit," said he, with a bitter smile; "heretofore it has been your purpose to make me govern for you, hereafter I shall govern for no one. If I shall, however, return to the throne of my fathers once more, you will be made to understand that I will profit by the experience you have given me[48]!"

[48] The king's own words. Mémoires d'une Femme de Qualité, vol. i. p. 156.

A few hours later, at nightfall, supported on the arm of Count Blacas, without any suite, and preceded by a single lackey bearing a torch, the king left the once more desolate and solitary Tuileries, and fled to Holland.

Twenty-four hours later, on the evening of the 20th of March, Napoleon entered the Tuileries, accompanied by the exulting shouts of the people, and the thundering *"Vive l'empereur"* of the troops. On the same place where the white flag of the Bourbons had but yesterday fluttered, the *tricolore* of the empire now flung out its folds to the breeze.

In the Tuileries the emperor found all his old ministers, his generals, and his courtiers, assembled. All were desirous of seeing and greeting him. An immense concourse of people surged around the entrance on the stairways and in the halls.

Borne aloft on the arms and shoulders of the people, the emperor was carried up the stairway, and into his apartments; and, while shouts of joy were resounding within, the thousands without joined the more fortunate ones who had borne the emperor to his apartments, and rent the air with exulting cries of "*Vive l'empereur!*"

In his cabinet, to which Napoleon immediately repaired, he was received by Queen Julia, wife of Joseph Bonaparte, and Queen Hortense, who had abandoned her place of concealment, and hurried to the Tuileries to salute the emperor.

Napoleon greeted Hortense coldly, he inquired briefly after the health of her sons, and then added, almost severely: "You have placed my nephews in a false position, by permitting them to remain in the midst of my enemies."

Hortense turned pale, and her eyes filled with tears. The emperor seemed not to notice it. "You have accepted the friendship of my enemies," said he, "and have placed yourself under obligations to the Bourbons. I depend on Eugene; I hope he will soon be here. I wrote to him from Lyons."

This was the reception Hortense received from the emperor. He was angry with her for having remained in France, and at the same time the flying Bourbons, who were on their way to Holland, said of her: "The Duchess of St. Leu is to blame for all! Her intrigues alone have brought Napoleon back to Paris."

CHAPTER XII
THE HUNDRED DAYS

The hundred days that followed the emperor's return are like a myth of the olden time, like a poem of Homer, in which heroes destroy worlds with a blow of the hand, and raise armies out of the ground with a stamp of the foot; in which nations perish, and new ones are born within the space of a minute.

These hundred days stand in history as a giant era, and these hundred days of the restored empire were replete with all the earth can offer of fortune, of magnificence, of glory, and of victory, as well as of all that the earth contains that is disgraceful, miserable, traitorous, and perfidious.

Wondrous and brilliant was their commencement. All France seemed to hail the emperor's return with exultation. Every one hastened to assure him of his unchangeable fidelity, and to persuade him that they had only obeyed the Bourbons under compulsion.

The old splendor of the empire once more prevailed in the Tuileries, where the emperor now held his glittering court again. There was, however, this difference: Queen Hortense now did the honors of the court, in the place of the Empress Marie Louise, who had not returned with her husband; and the emperor could not now show the people his own son, but could only point to his two nephews, the sons of Hortense.

The emperor had quickly reconciled himself to the queen; he had been compelled to yield to her gentle and yet decided explanations; he had comprehended that Hortense had sacrificed herself for her children, in continuing to remain in France notwithstanding her reluctance. After this reconciliation had taken place, Napoleon extended his hand to Hortense, with his irresistible smile, and begged her to name a wish, in order that he might fulfil it.

Queen Hortense, who had been so bitterly slandered and scorned by the royalists, and who was still considered by the fleeing Bourbons to be the cause of their overthrow--this same queen now entreated the emperor to permit the Duchess d'Orleans, who had not been able to leave Paris on account of a broken limb, to remain, and to accord her a pension besides. She told the emperor that she had received a letter from the duchess, in which she begged for her intercession in obtaining some assistance from the emperor, assuring her that it was urgently Deeded, in her depressed circumstances.

The emperor consented to grant this wish of his step-daughter Hortense; and it was solely at her solicitation that Napoleon accorded a pension of four hundred thousand francs to the Duchess d'Orleans, the mother of King Louis Philippe[49].

[49] La Reine Hortense en Italie, en France, et en Angleterre. Ecrit par elle-même, p. 185.

A few days later, at Hortense's request, a pension of two hundred thousand francs was also accorded to the Duchess of Bourbon, who had also besought the queen to exert her influence in her behalf; and both ladies now hastened to assure Hortense of their everlasting gratitude. The fulfilment of her wish filled Hortense with delight; she was as proud of it as of a victory achieved.

"I considered it a sacred duty," said she, "to intercede for these ladies. They were as isolated and desolate as I had been a few clays before, and I know how sad it is to be in such a state!"

But Hortense's present state was a very different one. She was now no longer the Duchess of St. Leu, but the queen and the ornament of the court once more; all heads now bowed before her again, and the high-born ladies, who had seemed oblivious of her existence during the past year, now hastened to do homage to the queen.

"Majesty," said one of these ladies to the queen, "unfortunately, you were always absent in the country when I called to pay my respects during the past winter."

The queen's only response was a gentle "Indeed madame," which she accompanied with a smile.

Hortense, as has before been said, was now again the grand point of attraction at court, and, at Napoleon's command, the public officials now also hastened to solicit the honor of an audience, in order to pay their respects to the emperor's step-daughter. Each day beheld new *fêtes* and ceremonies.

The most sublime and imposing of all these was the ceremony of the *Champ de Mai*, that took place on the first of June, and at which the emperor, in the presence of the applauding populace, presented to his army the new eagles and flags, which they were henceforth to carry into battle instead of the lilies of the Bourbons.

It was a wondrous, an enchanting spectacle to behold the sea of human beings that surged to and fro on this immense space, and made the welkin ring with their "*Vive l'empereur!*"--to behold the proud, triumphant soldiers receiving from Napoleon the eagles consecrated by the priests at the altar that stood before the emperor. It was a wondrous spectacle to behold the hundreds of richly-attired ladies glittering with diamonds, who occupied the tiers of seats that stood immediately behind the emperor's chair, and on which Hortense and her two sons occupied the first seats.

The air was so balmy, the sun shone so lustriously over all this splendor and magnificence, the cannon thundered so mightily, and the strains of music resounded so sweetly on the ear; and, while all were applauding and rejoicing, Hortense sat behind the emperor's chair covertly sketching the imposing scene that lay before her, the grand ceremony, which, a dark foreboding told her, "might perhaps be the last of the empire[50]."

[50] Cochelet, vol. iii., p. 97.

Hortense alone did not allow herself to be deceived by this universal delight and contentment.

The heavens still seemed bright and serene overhead, but she already perceived the gathering clouds, she already heard the mutterings of the storm that was soon, and this time forever, to hurl the emperor's throne to the ground. She knew that a day would suddenly come when all this brightness would grow dim, and when all those who now bowed so humbly before him, would turn from him again--a day when they would deny and desert the emperor as they had already done once before, and that, from that day on, the present period of grandeur would be accounted to her as a debt. But this knowledge caused her neither anxiety nor embarrassment.

The emperor was once more there; he was the lord and father left her by her mother Josephine, and it was her duty and desire to be true and obedient to him as long as she lived.

The sun still shone lustrously over the restored empire, and in the parlors of Queen Hortense, where the diplomats, statesmen, artists, and all the notables of the empire were in the habit of assembling, gayety reigned supreme. There music and literature were discussed, and homage done to all the fine arts.

Benjamin Constant, who had with great rapidity transformed himself from an enthusiastic royalist into an imperial state-councillor, came to the queen's parlors and regaled her guests by reading to them his romance Adolphe; and Metternich, the Austrian ambassador seemed to have no other destiny than to amuse the queen and the circle of ladies assembled around them, and to invent new social games for their entertainment.

Metternich knew how to bring thousands of charming little frivolities into fashion; he taught the ladies the charming and poetic language of flowers, and made it a symbolic means of conversation and correspondence in the queen's circle. He also, to the great delight of the court, invented the alphabet of gems; in this alphabet each gem represented its initial letter, and, by combinations, names and devices were formed, which were worn in necklaces, bracelets, and rings.

The little games with which the diplomatic Metternich occupied himself during the hundred days at the imperial court at Paris, were, it appears, of the most innocent and harmless nature.

CHAPTER XIII
NAPOLEON'S LAST ADIEU

The storm, of the approach of which Queen Hortense had so long had a foreboding, was preparing to burst over France. All the princes of Europe who had once been Napoleon's allies had now declared against him. They all refused to acknowledge Napoleon as emperor, or to treat with him as one having any authority.

"No peace, no reconciliation with this man," wrote the Emperor Alexander to Pozzo di Borgo; "all Europe is of the same opinion concerning him. With the exception of this man, any thing they may demand; no preference for any one; no war after this man shall have been set aside[51]."

[51] Cochelet, vol. iii., p. 90.

But, in order to "set this man aside," war was necessary. The allied armies therefore advanced toward the boundaries of France; the great powers declared war against France, or rather against the Emperor Napoleon; and France, which had so long desired peace, and had only accepted the Bourbons because it hoped to obtain it of them, France was now compelled to take up the gauntlet.

On the 12th of June the emperor left Paris with his army, in order to meet the advancing enemy. Napoleon himself, who had hitherto gone into battle, his countenance beaming with an assurance of victory, now looked gloomy and dejected, for he well knew that on the fate of his army now depended his own, and the fate of France.

This time it was not a question of making conquests, but of saving the national independence, and it was the mother-earth, red with the blood of her children, that was now to be defended.

Paris, that for eighty days had been the scene of splendor and festivity, now put on its mourning attire. All rejoicings were at an end, and every one listened hopefully to catch the first tones of the thunder of a victorious battle.

But the days of victory were over; the cannon thundered, the battle was fought, but instead of a triumph it was an overthrow.

At Waterloo, the eagles that had been consecrated on the first of June, on the *Champ de Mai*, sank in the dust; the emperor returned to Paris, a fugitive, and broken down in spirit, while the victorious allies were approaching the capital.

At the first intelligence of his return, Hortense hastened to the Elysée, where he had taken up his residence, to greet him. During the last few days she had been a prey to gloomy thoughts; now that the danger had come, now when all were despairing, she was composed, resolute, and ready to stand at the emperor's side to the last.

Napoleon was lost, and Hortense knew it; but he now had most need of friends, and she remained true, while so many of his nearest friends and relatives were deserting him.

On the twenty-second day of June the emperor sent in his abdication in favor of his son, the King of Rome, to the chambers; and a week later the chambers proclaimed Napoleon's son Emperor of France, under the name of Napoleon II.

But this emperor was a child of four years, and was, moreover, not in France, but in the custody of the Emperor of Austria, whose army was now marching on Paris with hostile intent!

Napoleon, now no longer Emperor of France, had been compelled to take the crown from his head a second time; and for the second time he quitted Paris to await the destiny to be appointed him by the allies.

This time he did not repair to Fontainebleau, but to Malmaison-- to Malmaison, that had once been Josephine's paradise, and where her heart had at last bled to death. This charming resort had passed into the possession of Queen Hortense; and Napoleon, who but yesterday had ruled over a whole empire, and to-day could call nothing, not even the space of ground on which he stood, his own, Napoleon asked Hortense to receive him at Malmaison.

Hortense accorded his request joyfully, and, when her friends learned this, and in their dismay and anxiety conjured her not to identify in this manner herself and children with the fate of the emperor, but to consider well the danger that would result from such a course, the queen replied resolutely: "That is an additional reason for holding firm to my determination. I consider it my sacred duty to remain true to the emperor to the last, and the greater the danger that threatens the emperor, the happier I shall be in having it in my power to show him my entire devotion and gratitude."

And when, in this decision, when her whole future hung in the balance, one of her most intimate lady-friends ventured to remind the queen of the disgraceful and malicious reports that had once been put in circulation with regard to her relation to Napoleon, and suggested that she would give new strength to them by now receiving the emperor at Malmaison, Hortense replied with dignity: "What do I care for these calumnies? I fulfil the duty imposed on me by feeling and principle. The emperor has always treated me as his child; I shall therefore ever remain his devoted and grateful daughter; it is my first and greatest necessity to be at peace with myself[52]."

[52] Cochelet, vol. iii., p. 149.

Hortense therefore repaired with the emperor to Malmaison, and the faithful, who were not willing to leave him in his misfortune, gathered around him, watched over his life, and gave to his residence a fleeting reflection of the old grandeur and magnificence. For they who now stood around Napoleon, guarding his person from any immediate danger that threatened him at the hands of fanatic enemies or hired assassins, were marshals, generals, dukes, and princes.

But Napoleon's fate was already decided--it was an inevitable one, and when the intelligence reached Malmaison that the enemy was approaching nearer and nearer, and that resistance was no longer made anywhere, and when Napoleon saw that all was lost, his throne, his crown, and even the love which he imagined he had for ever built up for himself in the hearts of the French people by his great deeds and victories--when he saw this he determined to fly, no matter whither, but away from the France that would no longer rally to his call, the France that had abandoned him.

The emperor resolved to fly to Rochefort, and to embark there in order to return to Elba. The provisional government that had established itself in Paris, and had sent an ambassador to Napoleon at Malmaison with the demand that he should depart at once, now instructed this ambassador to accompany the emperor on his journey, and not to leave him until he should have embarked.

Napoleon was ready to comply with this demand. He determined to depart on the afternoon of the 30th of June. He had nothing more to do but to take leave of his friends and family. He did this with cold, tearless composure, with an immovable, iron countenance; no muscle of his face quivered, and his glance was severe and imperious.

But, when Hortense brought in her two sons, when he had clasped them in his arms for the last time, then a shadow passed over his countenance; then his pale compressed lips quivered, and he turned away to conceal the tears that stood in his eyes.

But Hortense had seen them, and in her heart she preserved the remembrance of these tears as the most precious gem of her departed fortune. As the emperor then turned to her to bid her adieu in his former cold and immovable manner, Hortense, who well knew that a volcano of torments must be glowing under this cold lava, entreated him to grant her a last favor.

A painful smile illumined the emperor's countenance for a moment. There was, it seemed, still something that he could grant; he was not altogether powerless! With a mute inclination of the head he signified his assent. Hortense handed him a broad black belt.

"Sire," said she, "wear this belt around your body and beneath your clothing. Conceal it carefully, but in the time of necessity remember it and open it."

The emperor took the belt in his hand, and its weight startled him.

"What does it contain?" asked he: "I must know what it contains!"

"Sire," said Hortense, blushing and hesitating: "Sire, it is my large diamond necklace that I have taken apart and sewed in this belt. Your majesty may need money in a critical moment, and you will not deny me this last happiness, your acceptance of this token."

The emperor refused, but Hortense entreated him so earnestly that he was at last compelled to yield, and accept this love-offering.

They then took a hasty and mute leave of each other, and Hortense, in order to hide her tears, hastened with her children from the room.

The emperor summoned a servant, and ordered that no one else should be admitted; but at this moment the door was hastily thrown open, and a national guard entered the room.

"Talma!" exclaimed the emperor, almost gayly, as he extended his hand.

"Yes, Talma, sire," said he, pressing the emperor's hand to his lips. "I disguised myself in this dress, in order that I might get here to take leave of your majesty."

"To take leave, never to see each other more," said the emperor, sadly. "I shall never be able to admire you in your great *rôles* again, Talma. I am about to depart, never to return again. You will play the emperor on many an evening, but not I, Talma! My part is at an end!"

"No, sire, you will always remain the emperor!" exclaimed Talma, with generous enthusiasm; "the emperor, although without the crown and the purple robe."

"And also the emperor without a people," said Napoleon.

"Sire, you have a people that will ever remain yours, and a throne that is imperishable! It is the throne that you have erected for yourself on the battle-fields, that will be recorded in the books of history. And every one, no matter to what nation he may belong, who reads of your great deeds, will be inspired by them, and will acknowledge himself to be one of your people, and bow down before the emperor in reverence."

"I have no people," murmured Napoleon, gloomily; "they have all deserted--all betrayed me, Talma!"

"Sire, they will some day regret, as Alexander of Russia will also one day regret, having deserted the great man he once called brother!" And, in his delicate and generous endeavor to remind Napoleon of one of his moments of grandeur, Talma continued: "Your majesty perhaps remembers that evening at Tilsit, when the Emperor of Russia made you so tender a declaration of his love, publicly and before the whole world? But no, you cannot remember it; for you it was a matter of no moment; but I--I shall never forget it! It was at the theatre; we were playing 'Oedipus.' I looked up at the box in which your majesty sat, between the King of Prussia and the Emperor Alexander. I could see you only--the second Alexander of Macedon, the second Julius Caesar--and I held my arms aloft and saw you only when I repeated the words of my part: 'The friendship of a great man is a gift of the gods!' And as I said this, the Emperor Alexander arose and pressed you to his heart. I saw this, and tears choked my utterance. The audience applauded rapturously; this applause was, however, not for me, but for the Emperor Alexander[53]!"

[53] This scene is entirely historical. See Bossuet, Mémoires; Bourrienne, Mémoires; Cochelet and Une Femme de Qualité.

While Talma was speaking, his cheeks glowing and his eyes flashing, a rosy hue suffused the emperor's countenance, and, for an instant, he smiled. Talma had attained his object; he had raised up the humiliated emperor with the recital of his own grandeur.

Napoleon thanked him with a kindly glance, and extended his hand to bid him adieu.

As Talma approached the emperor, a carriage was heard driving up in front of the house. It was Letitia, the emperor's mother, who had come to take leave of her son. Talma stood still, in breathless suspense; in his heart he thanked Providence for permitting him to witness this leave-taking.

"Madame mère" walked past Talma in silence, and without observing him. She saw only her son, who stood in the middle of the room, his sombre and flashing glance fastened on her with an unutterable expression. Now they stood face to face, mother and son. The emperor's countenance remained immovable as though hewn out of marble.

They stood face to face in silence, but two great tears slowly trickled down the mother's cheeks. Talma stood in the background, weeping bitterly. Napoleon remained unmoved. Letitia now raised both hands and extended them to the emperor. "Adieu, my son!" said she, in full and sonorous tones.

Napoleon pressed her hands in his own, and gazed at her long and fixedly; and then, with the same firmness, he said: "My mother, adieu!"

Once more they gazed at each other; then the emperor let her hand fall. Letitia turned to go, and at this moment General Bertrand appeared at the door to announce that all was prepared for the journey[54].

[54] This leave-taking was exactly as above described, and Talma himself narrated it to Louise de Cochelet. See her Mémoires, vol. iii, P. 173.